THE MAN WITH THE SAWED-OFF LEG

AND OTHER TALES OF A NEW YORK CITY BLOCK

DANIEL J. WAKIN

Arcade Publishing · New York

To Vera, Thomas, and Michael
And the memory of my parents
A history: Past, present, and future

First paperback edition 2019

Arcade Publishing books may be purchased in bulk at special discounts for sales promotion, corporate gifts, fund-raising, or educational purposes. Special editions can also be created to specifications. For details, contact the Special Sales Department, Arcade Publishing, 307 West 36th Street, 11th Floor, New York, NY 10018 or arcade@skyhorsepublishing.com.

Arcade Publishing® is a registered trademark of Skyhorse Publishing, Inc.®, a Delaware corporation.

Visit our website at www.arcadepub.com.

10 9 8 7 6 5 4 3 2 1

Library of Congress Cataloging-in-Publication Data:
Names: Watkin, Daniel J., author.
Title: The Man with the Sawed-Off Leg and other tales of a New York City Block / Daniel J. Watkin.
Description: First Arcade edition. | New York : Arcade Publishing, 2018.
Identifiers: LCCN 2017045561 (print) | LCCN 2017053917 (ebook) | ISBN 9781628728491 (ebook) | ISBN 9781628728453 (hardcover : alk. paper) | ISBN 9781948924511 (paperback)
Subjects: LCSH: Upper West Side (New York, N. Y.) --History --Anecdotes | Upper West Side (New York, N. Y.) --Biography --Anecdotes | New York (N. Y.) --History --Anecdotes | New York (N. Y.) --Biography --Anecdotes
Classification: LCC F128.68.U67 W34 2018 (print) | DDC 974.7/1 [B]
LC record available at https://lccn.loc.gov/2017045561

Cover design by Erin Seaward-Hiatt
Cover photo by Percy Loomis Sperr © Milstein Division,
The New York Public Library

Printed in the United States of America

Contents

Preface

SINCE THE PUBLICATION OF THE HARDCOVER edition of this book, a number of important sources have emerged which merit mining for this paperback version. The new edition also allows for the correction of an error dating back to 1903, when an anonymous New York City clerk recorded Julia Marlowe's purchase of a house. The address, written in a loopy script in mortgage and property transfer records from that year and repeated later, was incorrectly listed as 337 Riverside Drive, instead of 335 Riverside Drive, an error that persisted in the city's annals for more than a century. (Mary Donnell received the same treatment, her address inadvertently changed from No. 333 to No. 335.)

Attentive readers alerted me to sources that enriched the story of 335 Riverside—namely, published recollections by members of the Faber family about Lothar Faber, the pencil patriarch, and what life was like in his teeming household. And most delightfully, descendants of Bennie the Bum, the man with the sawed-off leg, recognized him as their shady and hazily remembered Uncle Bernard, who had dropped out of the family. Mystery solved.

Dramatis Personae

The Rubel Gangsters
John "Fats" Manning, West Sider, rumrunner
Bernard "Bennie the Bum" McMahon, same, in "Legs" Diamond's circle
John Oley, Albany mobster
Francis Oley, his brother
Percy "Angel Face" Geary, Albany mobster
John J. "Archie" Stewart, loudmouth middleman
Stewart "One Arm" Wallace, gang recruit
Thomas Quinn, boatman
John Hughes, boatman
Joseph Kress, car thief and driver

Plus:
Madeline Tully, boardinghouse operator
Dr. Harry Gilbert, underworld doctor

Armored Car Guards
William Lilienthal
John Wilson
Joseph Allen

The Trial, June 26–July 13, 1939

William O'Dwyer, judge. Later mayor of New York.

William F. X. Geoghan, Brooklyn district attorney

Hyman Barshay, prosecutor

Burton Turkus, lawyer for Stewart Wallace

Caesar Barra, lawyer for Thomas Quinn

Vincent Impellitteri, lawyer for Joseph Kress and another future mayor

John Osnato, a lead detective

Albany Kidnapping, July 7, 1939

Daniel O'Connell, Albany political boss

John "Solly" O'Connell, his brother

John "Butch" O'Connell, Solly's son and a National Guard lieutenant

Manny Strewl, Oley associate and go-between with the kidnappers

The Seven Beauties

330 RIVERSIDE DRIVE

Robert Benson Davis, or R. B., the baking powder king

Jennie Davis, his wife

Lucretia Davis, or Lulu, their daughter and heir to the building

George S. Jephson, Lulu's husband

331 RIVERSIDE DRIVE

William P. Ahnelt, fashion magazine pioneer

Marion Davies, actress and mistress of William Randolph Hearst

Introduction

IN THE WANING LIGHT OF AN August evening in 1934, three men climbed up the stoop of a townhouse at 334 Riverside Drive, between 105th and 106th streets on Manhattan's Upper West Side. The building revealed pretensions to elegance from another era in its columns flanking a rounded arch over the entrance, carved stone ornamentation, and filigreed wrought iron balconies. Now it was a seedy rooming house under the care of one Madeline Tully, who catered to prostitutes and individuals in need of temporary disappearance. That night, the men carried a companion, his left pant leg soaked with blood. He was called Bennie the Bum, more formally known as Bernard McMahon, and he had had the misfortune of accidentally blasting himself in the knee with a sawed-off shotgun while motoring in a speedboat across the gray waters of Gravesend Bay off Brooklyn. Bennie, it seems, had been trying to untangle the gun from a rope in the bottom of the boat. McMahon was no expert at nautical tasks. His skills lay in driving trucks, loading crates of liquor, and knocking heads together as a former bootlegger and enforcer for the dapper gangster Jack "Legs" Diamond.

In the bottom of the boat were canvas bags, stuffed with hundreds of thousands of dollars just liberated from an armored car.

Until the misguided shotgun blast, everything had gone smoothly on that sultry Tuesday, August 21, 1934. The armored car made a stop at the Rubel Ice Company warehouse in Brooklyn's Bath Beach section, and there Bennie and his companions robbed it of $427,950 in what was then the most lucrative armored car heist in United States history. The operation—spectacular, daring, and meticulously planned—was carried out by an ad hoc gang composed of former bootleggers, toughs from Manhattan's West Side docks, and gangsters from Albany. They vanished in minutes, making an unusual escape by water over the bay. Half of them aboard a motorboat and the other half in a lobster dory, they curved east around a thumb of land called Seagate, then past Breezy Point at the end of the Rockaways strip. They shot through Rockaway Inlet, between mainland Brooklyn and the strip, and into Jamaica Bay. The men dumped their guns overboard, landed on the barrier island, and scuttled their boats. Four headed back to Manhattan by bus and subway. Two drove to a safe house in Queens. The other three procured a car to take the bleeding McMahon to the refuge on Riverside Drive. There, they brought an underworld doctor who summarily amputated McMahon's damaged leg. Unfortunately, the Bum lost so much blood that several days later he was dead.

For a moment, let's leave behind the movie-quality drama of the robbery—and the greed, recklessness, and depravity displayed by its protagonists—and turn to stone, brick, and iron. Mr. McMahon's final stop, 334 Riverside Drive, is one of a row of seven buildings that predate the Great Depression by three decades, arising at the dawn of the twentieth century. A lovely line of Beaux-Arts townhouses, they face out onto Riverside Drive, their windows staring across Riverside Park through the trees and over the Hudson River into the rise that marks the beginning of New Jersey and the continental United States.

To the south, the row begins with No. 330 on the corner of 105th Street, the most elegant and refined of them all, a delightful Parisian lady of the Belle Epoque. Next, heading north, No. 331 and No. 333 are creamy near-identical twins. No. 332 is a gap in this urban smile, torn down sometime in the mid-twentieth century. No. 334 is a stodgy middle-aged uncle with a plainer face despite the columns and carvings. No. 335 is a slender maiden, red brick and white-trimmed with stately columns in front. No. 336 is the dullest of the lot, receding into the background next to the Dickensian-style River Mansion at No. 337, on the corner of 106th Street, a boldly designed structure with ivy-wreathed Victorian red brick, contrasting limestone ornaments, and wrought iron barricades. All are official New York City landmarks.

Like No. 334 and the bloody chapter it witnessed, each building in this phalanx of townhouses has served as its own stage set for events of the past—scandals, family feuds, betrayals, suicide, fortunes made and lost. The protagonists have been moguls and maids, artists and office-workers, proper burghers and petty thieves, a great scientist, a former slaveholder, and a famous kept woman. They include an extraordinary array of great names in American letters, arts, and industry, all brought together at one geographical point, right here on this quiet bit of sidewalk. It's possible that digging into the history of many blocks in New York would unearth an impressive roster of residents. But the epoch and location of these townhouses, and the nature and history of the neighborhood, make for a pretty amazing and unique confluence of people.

The stories of the earliest occupants bring to life the prosperous, vigorous New York City that existed in the toddler years of the twentieth century. Horse-pulled trolleys lurched down the streets and hansom cabs ferried the gentry to the sound of clip-clops. The subway was just making its tunneled arrival. Homes were heated with coal, indoor electric lighting was a relative novelty, and lamplighters lit up gas street lamps. Spittoons adorned many rooms, upper class women trussed themselves up with corsets and received visitors during at-home days, and gentlemen retreated to the library after dinner for cigars. Columbia University had recently been built just to the north in Morningside Heights, joining a collection of grand structures—the Cathedral Church of St. John the Divine, St. Luke's Hospital, and Grant's tomb among them.

Those early owners were men who came to New York City from elsewhere to pursue profit through commerce. Unlikely to be accepted by the four hundred families of old New York, the Fifth Avenue society so finely drawn by Edith Wharton, they wound up in the elegant wilds of Riverside Drive. They had recent roots in Europe or the Midwest. These men were self-made and carved out fortunes in industries like rubber tires, publishing, and brick making. Some of these businesses made items that, amazingly, are still part of our everyday lives. The families included the Fabers of the No. 2 pencil fame; the baking powder Davises, whose product is sold in familiar yellow and red containers; the Penfields, a branch of the Goodyear tire family; a toothpaste magnate whose brand still sells in Asia; one of the nation's earliest biotech entrepreneurs; and the German immigrant who helped invent the modern fashion magazine. In several buildings, the same families remained in residence for decades, some well into the 1950s. While Bennie the Bum was undergoing dismemberment in No. 334, the black sheep of the block, the Fabers in 335 and the Canavans, a construction business dynasty, in 333, were ensconced in their comfortable homes on either side. The Penfields and Lucretia Jephson, the Davis baking powder heir, also were carrying on with their routines.

Artistic New Yorkers lived there too, including Julia Marlowe, one of the great Shakespearean actresses of her day. A more populist performer also lived on the row: Marion Davies, the former chorine, film star, and mistress of the publishing magnate William Randolph Hearst. Some years later, Duke Ellington bought two of the buildings, and Saul Bellow grieved for the death of his father and wrote fiction there.

As I tooled down these paths, researching who lived in each building, the Rubel heist story burst out as the biggest and juiciest tale, one whose chapters played out far beyond a small building in one neighborhood of one borough in one metropolis. A single gruesome incident in the Rubel saga took place on Riverside Drive, but the whole story was too irresistible to stop there. So I followed the thread, through the archives of federal courts and Alcatraz prison and newspapers, through the streets and along the shoreline of Brooklyn, through the written record of crimefighting in New York City. A great story of 1930s New York emerged, an era of snap-brimmed hats, high-waisted baggy trousers, and an underworld dominated by the Irish.

Some of the gangsters who took part in the Rubel job were longstanding waterfront toughs. In the years that followed, several participants were murdered or disappeared mysteriously. Others were sent to Alcatraz for a celebrated Albany kidnapping, the subject of William Kennedy's novel *Billy Phelan's Greatest Game*, an elegiac book set in underworld Albany, a city where the political machine was just another racket.

A few of the Rubel gang did go on trial, in a case that brought together figures who would become prominent New Yorkers. Future Mayor William O'Dwyer was the judge. Another future mayor, Vincent Impellitteri—"Impy," irresistibly, to the tabloid headline writers—was a defense lawyer. Burton Turkus, who as a prosecutor dismantled Murder, Inc., the prototype of a mass-murdering criminal enterprise, also defended a member of the gang.

The heist was one of the most famous robberies of its time. The popular radio program "Gang Busters" devoted an episode to several of its protagonists. A film noir called *Armored Car Robbery* was based, extremely loosely, on the affair. The *New York Times* termed the robbery "a classic in modern criminal annals." Publications ranging from *Argosy*, the pulp magazine, to the *New Yorker* chronicled the case. (The *New Yorker* article, in two parts, was co-written by Jack Alexander, who later joined the *Saturday Evening Post* and in 1941 wrote the first major article about Alcoholics Anonymous, a piece credited with launching a worldwide movement and turning the author into a hero to AA members.)

And yet the Rubel robbery soon fell into oblivion.

This book attempts to resurrect that story and others. It results from a fascination with what might be called the biography of structure, the notion that buildings have life stories drawn from the flesh-and-blood beings who pass through them. Bennie's demise happened just twenty-seven years before I, newly born, came home from the hospital to a small two-bedroom apartment just around the corner from the room where the life had bled out of him. What's twenty-seven years? It seems so little compared to the chasm between the 1930s and now, the early years of the new millennium. My arrival, like Bennie's departure, was just another event in a dwelling on a block of the Upper West Side of Manhattan, but both are reminders that dwellings, like human beings, are vessels of memory. A succession of individuals flits through the rooms of buildings, playing out the dramas of existence: births and deaths, violent acts and domestic routines. The rooms remain, the walls stand, and the next wave of residents move in, unaware of their predecessors. The rhythm brings to mind the verse from Job 14:1–2 that is carved on the memorial to an "amiable child," St. Clair Pollack, who died at age five in 1797, and sits just a mile away in Riverside Park: "Man that is born of woman / is of few days and full / of trouble. He cometh / like a flower and is / cut down; He fleeth also / as a shadow and / continueth not." Here is a vivid example of the brevity of life compared to the longevity of buildings.

A strange paradox occurred to me. I had grown up around these buildings and walked by them so many times that they had become a routine part of my mental landscape. They were deeply familiar. Yet I knew nothing of the lives that were carried on within these walls. And some day one of those forgotten stories would be mine. Other people living in my home would wonder about the anonymous residents of generations past.

In 2000, I moved back into my childhood apartment around the corner from these wonderful memory banks of brick and stone. This time I was a husband and father of two sons of my own. Now the walls that contained my progress through childhood and adolescence would do the same for two other young men. Much had changed in my childhood home. The kind of renovation that was de rigueur for big Upper West Side rental buildings going co-op eliminated a long hallway once used for roller-skating. There were new built-in closets. The peeling paint blotches on the ceiling that formed animals when stared at were smoothed away. Old appliances—a black-and-white Zenith television set, the round-edged ice box, the crude pop-up toaster—were replaced with modern items. The red corduroy couch was gone.

The streetscape remained the same, especially the large apartment houses across the street visible through our row of windows, especially lovely after a snowfall, when white bands traced the lintels and pediments on the facade. So did the view west, where jagged ice chunks flow down the Hudson River in winter. The sound of shouts of children playing on the streets—mine when I was a child, now my own boys'—was also the same. The traffic of the West Side Highway still hummed in the dead of night. The *New York Times* still plopped on the doorstep early in the morning, only now I was on the paper's payroll. I had weird flashbacks created specifically by the physical surroundings when I saw one of our little sons yell "Ow!" from a splinter bestowed by the same floorboards, or when I watched him jump up to reach the same light switch.

Being back in my old home ignited memories: coming home from school, opening the door, and seeing my mother's graduate students in the living room, the result of Vietnam War protests shutting down Columbia University. Standing in the kitchen and hearing a string of firecrackers pop, which were really gunshots aimed at two police officers on Riverside Drive. Sitting on the edge of my mother's bed, watching the Nixon-Humphrey returns in 1968.

Other memories lurked behind the facade of 334 Riverside Drive, namely Bennie the Bum's mutilation. Now it was a quiet, familiar place to amble by with the dog or hurry past for Little League games in Riverside Park. For all those years, I was blithely unaware of the building's dark history, or of the stories of its neighbors, those townhouses I came to call the Seven Beauties, and their many inhabitants. But years later, once the lights of the past slowly blinked to life behind the windows of those houses, this idea tugged at me: What do we really know about the physical surroundings of our daily life? What are the events that occur and then vanish as if they never happened? How do we confront the rather clobbering idea that moments of such significance in our daily lives, our very lives themselves, will evaporate into nothingness while the walls still stand?

In the ensuing chapters, I'll be giving the forgotten inhabitants of the Seven Beauties their due as ensemble players in a twentieth-century New York City drama starring Bennie and company in the leading roles. Imagine the row of townhouses as a Grand Hotel, and this book a trip through the hallways with a peek into the lives of a large cast of hotel guests. Looked at another way, the story of the townhouses helps us understand just what is special about cities in general. The Grand Hotel guests may have known each other only slightly—or in most cases not at all—as they lived cheek by jowl, but their lives intersected in ways they may not even have realized. At the least they shared the same architectural landscape, the same urban geography. What is a city but a concentrated collection of individual stories?

The result of my research is a work that is one part true-crime drama, one part New York history, and one part insanely detailed walking tour of a single city block. It is also a story of New York in microcosm, from its rural origins as a Dutch settlement, through British takeover, division into estates and their breakups, land speculation, the building of neighborhoods, their flourishing and decline and eventual gentrification, and coagulation into the mix of poor, middle class, rich and capitalist and bohemian that makes the city so special today.

CHAPTER 1

The Planning, Stage 1: "Bags of Money"

PROHIBITION ARRIVED IN THE UNITED STATES on January 17, 1920, and with it came profound changes to American life. Women received the vote partly because of the alliance between suffragists and temperance advocates. Gangsterism ran rampant, and criminal syndicates of immense wealth and power arose to supply alcohol to the masses. A considerable amount of blood was spilled.

In this fertile ground for many Irish American gangsters, Bernard McMahon and John Manning, another key figure in the Rubel robbery, took part as bootleggers. "Many people of Irish descent saw the temperance movement and Prohibition as a direct assault on their very existence," T. J. English wrote in *Paddy Whacked: The Untold Story of the Irish American Gangster.* The movement took aim at a central place in Irish life—the saloon, a communal gathering spot—and a common occupation among Irish immigrants, the liquor business. Defying Prohibition was a "cultural duty," as English put it.

McMahon and Manning knew each other from earlier days on the docks along Manhattan's West Side, where they served as strong-arm help for labor racketeers who controlled much of the business of loading and unloading ships. Central to the enterprise at the time was the International Longshoremen's Association, a union where many gangsters cut their teeth. The Port of New York was an economic powerhouse. Thousands of ships passed through each year, and by the eve of World War II, the port handled about a third of the cargo coming and going into the United States, at a value of some $15 billion.

The ban on drink eventually proved decidedly unpopular, and repeal came in the form of the Twenty-first Amendment, ratified fully on December 5, 1933. Thus came the demise of the mob's cash cow, and the end of a good living for men like McMahon and his friend Manning. They had to seek income elsewhere, like so many of their breed. A new racket had to be found. Some chose kidnapping or bank robbery. Some took up numbers-running or hijacking. Others went back to the docks to grab a piece of the illegal cash pie there, such as loan shark-ing, gambling, and violence designed to keep longshoremen in line. Our West Side duo's search for income led them to Brooklyn on a summer day in 1934.

Manning, twenty-seven, was slender, which naturally led to his acquiring the nickname "Fats." With blond hair and horn-rimmed glasses, he had the innocent, soft-spoken manner of a seminarian.

During Prohibition, Manning had transported illegal booze and handled payments, but his arrest record was pure, and so were his ambitions: to retire quietly to a farm upstate and raise cattle, a bucolic vision inspired perhaps by his upbringing in a village in Ireland. Or maybe, like so many poor, city-bound people, he simply yearned for a little calm in the countryside. In any case, his fate turned out to be something quite different.

Manning's friend boasted a flashier criminal pedigree. Bennie the Bum McMahon was born in 1893, one of three brothers and two sisters, and grew up in various apartments in the West 20s in Manhattan. His father, also Bernard McMahon, and mother, Anna McKenna, had emigrated from County Monaghan in Ireland. His father was a bartender, a sometime profession of the younger Bernard. He was also a proud graduate of the Elmira Reformatory, a penal institution in upstate New York, sported blond slicked-back hair, intense blue eyes, and arrests for disorderly conduct, receiving stolen goods, and burglary. His mouth turned down into a sneer from pursed lips, his eyes were placed a little too close together, and his ears stuck out. He had the look of a schoolyard bully. He was also an alumnus of the mob run by "Legs" Diamond, one of the most flamboyant and famous gangsters of the Roaring Twenties. (McMahon's association with Diamond was before Diamond made it big, before his violent death in an Albany rooming house in 1931, and before the Roaring Twenties became the Mundane Thirties for Bennie the Bum.)

In his youth, McMahon was a rumrunner too, smuggling liquor into speakeasies during Prohibition. McMahon had had one of his brushes with the law eleven years before the Rubel case when federal Prohibition agents, disguised as butchers, visited John's Restaurant at 553 West 36th Street in Hell's Kitchen, the spawning place for Irish thugs on Manhattan's West Side, and arrested him and the proprietor, John Felske. Why was McMahon at the restaurant? What was he arrested for? What was his connection to Felske? Details in news reports are scant. But we do know that at the time McMahon lived at 885 Columbus Avenue near 104th Street—four long blocks east of Riverside Drive—and now the site of the Frederick Douglass Houses. By the time planning for the Rubel heist began, McMahon had turned to hijacking and earned his sobriquet of "Bum" thanks to minor jobs like what might be called the Great Pill Heist.

On January 6, 1933, McMahon and a partner, Frank Mosconi, hijacked a truckload of aspirin on Hudson Street in lower Manhattan. They grabbed the driver, Herman Heim, and stashed him on the roof of a Hell's Kitchen tenement. Both McMahon and Mosconi were arrested. Such was "Legs's" fame that, even in small police blotter items such as the one relating this case, McMahon was described as the last of the Diamond gang. In any event, the charge didn't stick. The truck driver said he could not identify McMahon as the man who robbed him, and the case was dropped.

McMahon and Manning were also associated with a loose-knit faction of robbers led by Charlie Yanowsky, who grew up in Jersey City. Yanowsky, the son of Russian Jewish immigrants, was a savvy, ruthless gangster who began his career ransacking freight train cars, scaling them by means of rope ladders. He had recently began working on the West Side of Manhattan, planning robberies and running a numbers game.

On that summer day the next year in Brooklyn, as McMahon and Manning strolled around Coney Island investigating the possibility of robbing a bath house, they were stopped by a more promising sight: an armored car belonging to United States Trucking, parked in front of a Brooklyn Trust Company branch on West 12th Street near Surf Avenue. The pair watched as guards carted out canvas bags stuffed with money and loaded them into the vehicle.

The sight of those bags was like the smell of a roast to a hungry dog, and so the pair changed plans. *Why not rob the bank*, they thought. They began going out to Coney Island every day to scout out the branch and plan escape routes. Manning went inside to talk to a bank official, ostensibly about opening an account.

A bank being a more ambitious target than a bathhouse, the pair decided to recruit reinforcements. Manning tapped John "Archie" Stewart, an acquaintance from the West Side docks. Stewart, thirty-four, was a well-dressed ex-convict with a long record dating back to a burglary conviction at age fifteen and one for armed robbery at eighteen, for which he was sentenced to seven and a half to fourteen years in prison. When he wasn't behind bars, Stewart was a jack-of-all-crimes. He ran speakeasies and crap games and kept book. He was a gambler, a beer runner, and a bootlegger. For several years he carried a gun while transporting the take from floating crap games on the West Side. Like several of his fellow Rubel gang members, he served briefly in the Navy at the end of World War I. He bragged about knowing the gangster Owney Madden and mob boss Lucky Luciano.

As it turned out, the choice of Stewart would not be a wise one for the gang.

Although the bank was the original target, the trio soon decided to focus on the United States Trucking vehicle. A getaway could go awry on the crowded streets around Surf Avenue; if a bystander should be accidentally killed, the robbers would risk the death penalty.

The company's large green trucks—seventy-five of them, with windows over an inch thick—were a familiar sight in the metropolitan area. On any given day, armored cars carried a total of $19 million through the streets of New York. Guards, many of them former military men, were required to be crack shots. In that spirit, United States Trucking boasted its own rifle range, and regular practice and recertifications were required. The age limit for guards was thirty, thus excluding paunchy retired police officers.

The guards were not told their routes until the morning they were scheduled to set out, and they often rotated through different crews. They were assigned out of US Trucking's headquarters at 44 Beaver Street, now offices of the city's Department of Transportation. The trucks themselves were state of the art. They were fitted with portholes to fire out of and slides that could be pulled down as far as the gun barrel to prevent outsiders from pushing a gun through the opening. A brake in the storage area cut off the ignition if a bandit should make his way into the driver's compartment; an additional porthole allowed guards in the back of the truck to shoot any hijacker who got into the front. In the end, the technical specifications sounded much more effective than they were.

As the planned heist grew more ambitious and complicated, so did the workforce. Stewart brought in an old partner in crime, Stewart Wallace, a fifty-one-year-old Sing Sing alum with convictions for forgery and grand larceny who had lost a hand in a car accident, earning him the nickname One Arm. The two men met on West 50th Street in Manhattan, just off Broadway. "I asked Wallace whether he'd be interested in a job of taking over the armored car," Stewart said later. "Wallace said he would be, but that he'd like to look over the armored truck himself."

The next day, Stewart brought Wallace, McMahon, and Manning together at Coney Island. "We waited around for a while and then went to Surf Avenue and saw the car outside the bank. We saw two men get out of the car and go into the bank with bags of money. We followed the car for several stops."

Back in Manhattan that evening, the four men gathered at 79th Street and Riverside Drive, just opposite Riverside Park. All felt that the cash looked ready for the plucking. "Manning said, 'This looks like money from home,' and the rest of us agreed with him," Stewart later said. But Manning thought they would need more help and suggested inviting others into the gang. "I said I knew Percy Geary and John Oley, that they were broke, and that I knew they'd like to go along on the job," Stewart said. Manning hesitated. He knew a little something about Geary and Oley. They were two of the most wanted men in the country.

As the stonemasons were finishing up work on our Beaux-Arts townhouses along Riverside Drive, and as the first owners were preparing to move in, John Joseph Oley was born on January 7, 1901, the son of Irish immigrants who lived on Orange Street in Albany. His father was a machinist for the railroad, which would later employ several of his brothers. At sixteen, after two years in high school, Oley enlisted in the Navy. The date was July 17, 1917, just three months after the United States entered World War I. He served a year and ten days, the last seven months aboard the USS *South Carolina*, a battleship that spent most of the war cruising up and down the Atlantic seaboard. He was discharged a seaman 2nd class.

There is some evidence that even before turning twenty-one, Oley had sway in the commingled Albany underworld of low-lifes and politicians. Orange Street, where he grew up, was just a block from Sheridan Avenue, home of the Sheridan Avenue Gang, and a place which William Kennedy, in his book *O Albany! Improbable City of Political Wizards, Fearless Ethnics, Spectacular Aristocrats, Splendid Nobodies, and Underrated Scoundrels*, described as the redoubt of a "band of Irish toughs who, by legend, guarded their turf rigorously and let no strangers pass through." Accounts in the *Knickerbocker Press* describe a head-banging brawl on February 18, 1921, outside a dance at the Union Hall. The affair was billed as a benefit for striking streetcar workers. The roughhousing began inside with the assault on a police officer named Stephen Donnelley. A group of young men forced Donnelley into a coatroom and beat him with brass knuckles. Police officers arrived and cleared out the hall, but soon the brawlers turned on the cops. Four young men were arrested and at their arraignment the next day, "politicians, little and big" showed up in court to support them, the *Knickerbocker Press* reported. One of the young men was named John Oley.

It's unclear if this was the same Oley who surfaced in Brooklyn more than a decade later. In the newspaper account, Oley is described as eighteen—he would actually have been twenty—and from Sheridan Avenue, not Orange Street. It's entirely possible that the *Press* got both Oley's age and his address wrong.

In any event, court records show that before his twenty-first birthday, our John Oley had served six months in the Albany County Penitentiary for burglary. Four months later, he was sent down to the federal penitentiary in Atlanta and served four years for larceny. On April 4, 1928, he was arrested for first-degree assault with intent to kill, but was acquitted at trial. The victim was one Joey Green, a small-time racketeer who survived a barrage of gunshots.

By the time of the Rubel job, Oley was a blustering tough guy with a wide chin and thick hair parted in the middle. His face hung down low, and something about it seemed out of proportion, as if the distance from his eyes to the tip of his nose was too short compared to the height of his forehead and the length of his jaw. Officially, he was an independent trucker.

In Albany, Oley lived with his wife, Agnes, a nurse; his brother William; and his father. Francis, another brother, lived on the same block. Francis was younger and appeared to be the straighter arrow. He played basketball at Albany High School and by all accounts was a popular guy there. Nevertheless, according to Kennedy, John and Francis "grew up to become the city's best-known homegrown criminals."

Oley, with an associate named Manny Strewl, headed an Albany crew that hijacked trucks, sold bootleg liquor, and robbed banks. Liquor flowed from Canada to New York City, making Albany a key point along the route and a place to reap big profits. Indeed, Oley provided well for his family. According to an FBI report dated August 24, 1937, "He has a very limited education but has given his parents and brothers a large amount of property and money, proceeds obtained through bootlegging." Despite only a year of high school, Oley was not dumb: he had an IQ of 108.

Oley and Strewl pulled various capers. On an October day in 1928, they impersonated Prohibition agents and tried to shake down a Hoosick Falls hotel owner named Elizabeth Grabowski, threatening to arrest her for serving alcohol unless she came up with $300. Given the number of law enforcement officials corrupted by the mob during Prohibition, it wasn't an outlandish request. Mrs. Grabowski stayed cool, snuck out of the house, and called the police. Oley and Strewl spent a year in the penitentiary.

Oley's gangster associates in Albany included Percy Geary, nicknamed Angel Face. Geary was skinny, a pencil-necked beanstalk of a man with a narrow face, reddish hair, crossed eyes, and supercilious smile. He had the ability to show a congenial side, but had little education and never held a legitimate job for long. He was born the same year as Oley, 1901, and lived a mile away on Irving Street. Geary was the fifth of eleven children, four of whom had died at young ages. His father, William, had an eighth-grade education and worked as a bricklayer. Geary's surviving siblings had stable adult lives. The men in the family worked as a contractor, fireman, bricklayer, truck driver, and railroad brakeman. Geary lived in the family home until he was thirty-one, when he married his wife, Josephine.

Geary also spent part of his childhood in New York City. He was a loner, although he attended church and Sunday school often enough to be confirmed and receive first communion. Because of many illnesses and absences, he survived school only through the fifth grade, which he completed at age fourteen. He worked as a messenger boy, a helper at a laundry and a florist, and in beer wholesaling. His largest salary was $50 a week.

Geary's first recorded arrest, for burglary, came when he was fifteen. At least half a dozen other arrests followed, mostly for burglary, breaking and entering, and gun charges. Before the Rubel job, he had spent eleven years, a third of his life up to that point, in prison.

Documents related to his assignment to the prison at Leavenworth, Kansas, in 1938 described Geary as "a habitual criminal of the most vicious type."

Archie Stewart may have claimed that bringing Oley and Geary in was his idea. But it is likely that McMahon, the Manhattan gangster, knew the Albany criminals through a key connection: "Legs" Diamond. The Oley brothers and Geary both worked with Jack "Legs" Diamond in the early 1930s.

The criminal escapades of John Oley and Percy Geary—the bootlegging, the burglaries, the shakedowns, and other activities—formed a prelude to something much bigger, a crime that captured headlines—and later inspired a major work of fiction—before the Rubel case seized the public's attention. In some ways this crime, a high-profile kidnapping, was a rehearsal for the detailed organizing that went into the armored car robbery: the differentiated roles, the precise timing, the intricate travel arrangements, the many moving parts. It made sense to bring in Oley and Geary for the Rubel endeavor. They had a good track record for that sort of thing.

CHAPTER 2.

Origins: "A Benefit to the Neighborhood"

I N LATE AUGUST 1664, FOUR BRITISH frigates and some two thousand military men serving Colonel Richard Nicolls, a forty-year-old Dutch-speaking Englishman, glided into lower New York Harbor. Nicolls, under the authority of James, Duke of York, arrived to take control of the New Netherland colony from the Dutch and soon engineered its surrender to the British crown. Nicolls was appointed governor of the territory and began dispensing land patents; in 1667–1668, he granted one for the land running from what is now West 89th Street north to West 107th Street, and roughly from what is now Central Park West to the Hudson River, to Isaac Bedloe, a city alderman and merchant who gave his name to Bedloe's Island, the future repository of the Statue of Liberty.

The Bedloe patent fell within a district that the Dutch called Bloemendael, or vale of flowers, after a town near Haarlem in the Netherlands, and termed Bloomingdale by the English. The Dutch had never settled the area, and for centuries it was probably the hunting ground for a nearby Native American tribe, the Weckquaesgeek, a branch of the Algonquians. An old Native American trail, expanded in the late 1600s to transport tobacco grown in the area, became known by the 1700s as the Bloomingdale Road. Wealthy families established country estates along the route, which was the main artery heading into the city on the western side of Manhattan.

Humphrey Jones bought a chunk of land from West 99th to West 107th Streets. His estate was anchored by the Humphrey Jones Homestead (also referred to as the Ann Rogers House after a later owner), a stone house dating back to before 1752. It was located west of what is now West End Avenue, between 101st and 102nd streets. Through the early 1800s, the surrounding area was empty and green and full of farmland. In an oft-quoted passage from his *A History of New York by Diedrich Knickerbocker*, Washington Irving described Bloemendael as "a sweet rural valley, beautiful with many a bright flower, refreshed by many a pure streamlet and enlivened here and there by a delectable Dutch cottage, sheltered under some sloping hill, and almost buried in some embowering trees."

Large institutions began moving in, among them an insane asylum where Columbia University now sits, and the Leake and Watts Orphanage, part of which still stands on the site of the Cathedral Church of St. John the Divine. By the mid-nineteenth century, several hotels were established for Manhattan residents seeking to escape the summer heat. An inkling of the changing nature of the neighborhood came in 1851, when the Hudson River Railroad put down tracks along the waterway.

With the end of the Civil War, Manhattan's population was growing, making the island ripe for development. The large estates became juicy targets for land developers. The 105th–106th Street parcel of the Rogers Farm was sold in 1864 to Augustus Whiting, a Newport socialite, after being subdivided into thirty-four lots. The price: $16,700, or about $240,000 today. The rest of the farm was also broken up. But what is now the densely populated Upper West Side remained a no-man's-land. "Craggy slopes, running streams, and malarial pools marked the bleak and rocky land," wrote Edwin G. Burroughs and Mike Wallace in *Gotham: A History of New York City to 1898.* "It was barely accessible to downtown civilization." A lone horsecar line only reached 84th Street; beyond that, travelers needed a stagecoach. Even as late as 1876, cows were still pasturing around 100th Street.

Around the same time, city planners decided to carve out open space for a narrow park along the river, extending from 72nd Street to around 130th Street. It was an imperfect site. Though providing impressive views of the Palisades cliffs across the Hudson, the area encompassed a long slope to the river, and the Hudson River Railroad tracks cut off access to the water. Nevertheless, the park was created following the vision of Frederick Law Olmsted between 1875 and 1910, with the tracks eventually hidden underground. Today, on a quiet night, lonely train whistles can still be heard in the blocks close to Riverside Park.

The planners also transformed Bloomingdale Road into a wide avenue called the Boulevard, which opened in 1869, and which in 1899 was renamed Broadway. In 1881 the northern extension of the 9th Avenue El ran along today's Columbus Avenue, allowing for even more development in the neighborhood. Still, growth was spotty. The first Riverside mansions started sprouting in the 1880s at the edge of an area that remained largely vacant except for a few lonely wood- or brick-frame houses, goats, and stables. Then the speculators arrived, hoping to attract the wealthy with elegant townhouses. The northward extension of the subway, which ran along Broadway and opened in 1904, along with a campaign by the *New York Herald* extolling the area, helped drive land speculation. Grand apartment houses rose on the avenues. Tenements filled in the side streets, and the groundwork was laid for the Upper West Side's supremely eclectic nature, a neighborhood of artists and businessmen, leftists and eccentrics, lowlifes and working stiffs. Peter Salwen, in his history, *Upper West Side Story,* called the area, with remarkable precision, a "quirky, sordid, hustling, grandiose, hopelessly *over*articulate hodgepodge of a neighborhood." The architecture was similarly exuberant in its variety, encompassing notes of the Art Deco, Beaux-Arts, neoclassical, Edwardian, Italian Renaissance, Georgian, Romanesque Revival and neo-Gothic styles—sometimes a fistful in one building. Back at the end of the nineteenth century, hopes that the 1893 World's Columbian Exposition would arise in Riverside Park also fueled a sense of civic betterment that lingered on in succeeding decades and led to monuments in the park, like the Soldiers and Sailors memorial, Grant's Tomb, and the statues of Samuel Tilden, General Franz Sigel, Lajos Kossuth, and Joan of Arc. (Chicago eventually won the exposition, and it became known as the Chicago World's Fair.) More institutions arrived in the last decade of the 1800s, including Columbia University and St. John the Divine.

Riverside Drive was seen as a potential rival to Fifth Avenue. In 1895, the *New York Times* gushed, "There is no boulevard in all the world that compares with Riverside Drive in natural beauty." In fact, there was no shortage of boosters. In 1899, the architect Clarence True, who bought land along the drive and built houses on it, published a volume presenting photographs of Riverside mansions and extolling the avenue's glories, declaring Riverside Drive "the most ideal home-site in the western hemisphere—the Acropolis of the world's second city." The *Herald*'s campaign included encomiums like this from 1890: The Upper West Side is "sure to become within the next twenty years, perhaps the location of the most beautiful residences in the world. The advantages of pure air and beautiful surroundings, glimpses of the New Jersey Hills at the end of each street, with the glitter of the Hudson between; the nearness of the parks and the accessibility of the district will be insurmountable factors in popularity." Any current resident can still attest to those charms.

While the reality would never match such grandiose descriptions, the wealthy did make their way to Riverside, where impressive houses were being built for them. Eight of those houses arose between 1899 and 1902, dressed in the elegantly tailored Beaux-Arts style redolent of Paris and Old World gentility. Born at the dawn of the American Century, these structures on Riverside Avenue (as it was officially called until formally renamed Riverside Drive in 1908) between 105th and 106th Streets had different architects and builders, but all were bound by covenants requiring them to be "a benefit to the neighborhood." Developers committed themselves to keep the manmade surroundings beautiful—a challenging task given that squatters abounded along the waterfront, together with stables, feed stores, coal storage depots, commercial piers, and those railroad tracks with the racket of spark-spewing trains and the stench of the pigs and cows they sent to slaughterhouses in the southern part of the island.

The buildings on Riverside Drive between 105th and 106th streets must have seemed new and fresh in a city of brownstones. They were clad in limestone and light-colored brick, adorned with bright awnings outside the windows to keep the rooms inside cool. Edith Wharton, in *The House of Mirth*—set in the decade before Nos. 330–337 Riverside were built—has the character Lily Bart glance at "the new brick and limestone house-fronts, fantastically varied in obedience to the American craving for novelty, but fresh and inviting with their awnings and flower-boxes" in a downtown street. It was a description easily applicable to Riverside.

The Riverside buildings came to life in two clumps. One developer, Joseph A. Farley, built Nos. 330, 331, 332, and 333, using the architecture firm of Janes & Leo, a frequent collaborator that was also building a row of townhouses around the corner on 105th Street and the glorious Dorilton apartment house on 71st and Broadway at about the same time. Perez M. Stewart, a former commissioner of buildings, built Nos. 334, 335, 336, and 337 with his partner, H. Ives Smith. The pair were a huge force in creating the Upper West Side neighborhood as we know it. In the 1890s, their firm erected more than 100 buildings on the swath between West End and Riverside Drive, from 75th to 107th streets.

For Nos. 334, 335, and 336, Stewart and Smith used the plans of Hoppin & Koen, a firm that also designed the old police headquarters on Vesey Street, a firehouse on West 43rd Street, and many other private homes. A different architect, the prominent Robert D. Kohn, designed No. 337, known as River Mansion. He was barely thirty years old. The men behind these buildings were among the first colonizers of the mid-northerly reaches of the island of Manhattan.

Kohn was born in 1870 in Manhattan. He graduated from City College in 1886, received an architecture degree from Columbia University four years later, and like most ambitious American architects studied from 1891 to 1895 at the École des Beaux-Arts in Paris, where he absorbed the elegant style that would infuse River Mansion and its neighbors. The mansion was one of his earliest commissions, along with No. 322 West 106th Street next door and Nos. 352 and 353 Riverside Drive. Kohn was also the associate architect, with Carrere &

Hastings, of the school of the New York Society for Ethical Culture at 2 West 64th Street and the apartment house at 33 Central Park West. He went on to design office and institutional buildings, and commercial structures such as warehouses and factories, as well as apartment houses.

Kohn was also one of the relatively few American architects to be influenced by the Vienna Secession movement. Buildings he designed in that style include the Seeman Bros. warehouse on Perry Street in Greenwich Village and the *New York Evening Post* building at 20 Vesey Street. In the 1920s, Kohn designed additions to Macy's department store and worked on Manhattan's cathedral of a synagogue, Temple Emanu-El on Fifth Avenue.

Farley, the developer of the southern group of our townhouses, was a major figure in the neighborhood's growth. His father was Terence Farley, a prominent builder and a former alderman connected to Tammany Hall and the Boss Tweed crowd. Starting in 1897, Joseph Farley built several dozen residential buildings, many of them between 105th and 108th Streets on the West Side. (His brothers James and John also were real estate developers.)

Building Nos. 330, 331, 332, and 333 required him to put up a large sum of money: $430,000, the equivalent of nearly $12 million these days. *The Real Estate Record and Builders' Guide*, the real property bible of the day, greeted the structures with considerable fanfare. The four buildings "represent all that is latest in fashionable dwelling construction, and are furnished with all the devices for insuring the convenience and comfort of their occupants," the *Record* said in its October 4, 1902, issue. The homes were designed, the publication continued, "with artistic correctness and finished with taste," and reflected what the *Record* called Farley's "ingenuity" in planning. One example: "the placing of handsome billiard rooms in the front of the sub-basements of the inner houses." The *Record* went on to praise the "magnificent views of the Hudson River and the Riverside Drive," a location described as "airy, cheerful and salubrious." The green verge between the service road in front of the buildings and Riverside Drive itself provided some seclusion, it said, and went on to say that continued "high class" improvement in the area meant they were a good investment.

Sadly the publication's optimistic language of 1902 ran at odds with reality. Housing was in a slump at the time, and Farley could not sell his four buildings. Deeply in debt, he declared bankruptcy just two months after the article appeared. The "latest in fashionable dwelling construction" were foreclosed upon and auctioned off in 1903. His woes were not over: on March 8, 1904, a policeman showed up at Farley's office and arrested him for larceny. He was accused of taking out a $20,000 loan from the Fifth National Bank and putting up worthless paper as collateral. A lawyer for the bank claimed that Farley, in applying for the loan, had lied about his property holdings. Farley's brother James came to court and put up the $10,000 bail, using his house at 3 East 71st Street as collateral.

But Joseph Farley was a scrapper and in May he struck back. After an appellate court ordered his release, Farley sued the bank officials for $50,000. He had backing for the action from the appellate court, which had declared that the police officer who arrested Farley and the magistrate who allowed the arrest deserved "severe condemnation" for acts that were "illegal and arbitrary." The court rejected the idea that Farley had committed "larceny," calling the transaction a loan on a note.

The bankruptcy proved just a blip on the block's luster. The speculation of Farley and Stewart and Smith had left a noble row of buildings facing a new park and a new century. They were soon to be peopled by wealthy manufacturers, self-made men, and one self-made woman.

CHAPTER 3.

The Kidnapping: "You Are His God Now"

NINETEEN-NINETEEN WAS SUPPOSED TO BE THE year the Democrats broke the Albany Republican machine, whose boss was William Barnes, the wealthy owner of the Albany *Evening Journal*. The election held that year was brutal, filled with allegations of chicanery, and in the end the Republicans swept local offices. But the seed for their eventual demise was planted. A Navy veteran of Irish stock named Daniel O'Connell won barely enough votes to take one of the few positions captured by the Democrats: city tax assessor. This was the only elected job he would ever hold. But his political power became supreme.

O'Connell went on to become chairman of the Democratic Committee of Albany and thus the satrap of one of the most powerful political machines in the nation. "The tenacity of the Machine he built in those years is unique in the history of the country," William Kennedy wrote of the figure who held sway until his death in 1977 at ninety-one. "Since the early 1920s the O'Connell Machine had swept almost all city and county offices, held control of the county legislature and all local seats in the State Senate and Assembly."

The O'Connell empire included the Hedrick Brewing Company, which Dan O'Connell and his brother John, known as Solly, had a stake in. Solly was also linked to Albany-area gambling operations and was effectively the family's connection to the underworld. In 1933, Solly's son John was managing distribution for the brewing company, which had re-emerged into legitimacy with the repeal that year of Prohibition.

John, or Butch, as he was known, was twenty-four, an imposing, 225-pound lieutenant in the National Guard and the scion of the O'Connell family. He lived with his father, blocks away from Daniel and two other O'Connell brothers in Albany. On July 7 of that year, an hour past midnight, Butch pulled up in front of his two-story wooden house, where a widow's walk topped a small colonnaded porch over the front door. He was coming home from a date.

As O'Connell's car came to a stop, a man was waiting. He yanked open the passenger door, jumped in, pushed O'Connell out of the driver's side, and walloped him with a gun. With the help of an accomplice, he tied up O'Connell, blindfolded him, and shoved him into a new Pontiac sedan parked nearby. Then the trio drove off to New Jersey.

The man who pistol-whipped O'Connell that night was Percy Geary and his accomplice was John Oley, who was celebrating his thirty-second birthday. Together with Oley's bootlegging partner, Manny Strewl, they had come up with a brazen plan to kidnap a member of the city's most powerful political family. The memory of the kidnapping of the Lindbergh baby, despite the crime's disastrous outcome, was fresh in their minds. And with the repeal of Prohibition, a new source of income was needed; robbing armored cars was, in fact, only one option.

To carry out the kidnapping of Butch O'Connell, Geary and Oley had needed capital. Bank robbery was deemed the answer.

Before snatching their prey, Geary had arranged a meeting to discuss such a heist with Leonard Scarnici, a Springfield, Massachusetts-born hitman for "Legs" Diamond and fellow gangster Waxey Gordon. (Scarnici was in the employ of Dutch Schulz for his most celebrated murder: that of Vincent "Mad Dog" Coll, himself a practitioner of murder for hire, who was slain in a hail of machine-gun bullets while inside a phone booth on West 23rd Street in Manhattan on February 8, 1932.)

In May of 1933, Scarnici and his men held up a bank in the city of Rensselaer, New York, across the Hudson River from Albany, to raise money for the kidnapping. In the course of the robbery, someone tripped a silent alarm. Two policemen responded, and a bloodbath ensued. Two of Scarnici's men were killed, but so was Detective James Stevens. The take was a measly $2,000.

Scarnici was the only suspect identified, and he was arrested, tried, convicted, and executed for the crime, chewing gum and smoking a cigarette on his way to the death chamber. Scarnici's final words were reported to be, "All I want to say to those double-crossers up in Albany is that I'm a better man than they are." The "double-crossers" were believed to be Geary and Oley; something, apparently, did not please Scarnici about their business arrangement.

With Scarnici out of the picture, new muscle was needed for the kidnapping job. Strewl made contact with Charles Harrigan, the leader of a gang in Hoboken, New Jersey. With the take from the bank robbery money, a henchman bought a used Durant Coupe from an Albany car dealer. The purchase was merely a way to obtain a legitimate license plate, which was then removed from the Durant and attached to the Pontiac sedan to which O'Connell was first transferred. After grabbing O'Connell, the gang took to the road and switched vehicles, pulling over to be met by a car-transporter truck driven by a confederate. O'Connell was stuffed into a secret compartment between the cab and a false back of the cargo section. Two members of the Hoboken crew climbed in and drove the truck to a rented apartment in Hoboken and stashed the kidnap victim there, where he remained handcuffed to the bed for three weeks. One man was assigned to bring his meals. Three others kept twenty-four-hour guard.

Harrigan periodically visited the apartment and had O'Connell sign several blank sheets of paper. Over the next three weeks, the gang delivered ten letters to an Albany post office box and the Beaver Clothing Company in Albany, making their demands to O'Connell's family. The initial demand, sent to Edward O'Connell, a lawyer and John O'Connell's uncle, was for $250,000 in exchange for the life of his nephew. Otherwise, the letter promised, his body would never be found. Two of the letters were typed, three were written by O'Connell himself, and five were handwritten by someone else above his signature.

The handwritten letters are still in the court file, folded pieces of notepaper stapled to the envelopes. Trial exhibit numbers are written on the notes. "Dan," began one addressed to John's uncle, Daniel O'Connell, handwritten in capital letters. "If this is made public it is the *end*. All negotitations [sic] must be secret or it is curtains for John. No letter is genuine unless it contains Johns [sic] signature. This will be ended fast if you get the *sugar up* and no kidding us." The letter continued, "You are his God *now* and his only hope to live. *So play fair and we will do likewise.*" The kidnappers showed some psychological sophistication by trying to give O'Connell—the corrupt machine politician par excellence—a way to identify with them: "You have *your racket* and you can be thankful it *gave you plenty*, and we have ours."

One letter told the O'Connells to insert, each day, a list of the names of Albany racketeers in the local paper. The kidnappers said they would choose a name from the list as an intermediary who would pay the ransom and pick up O'Connell. (As Frank S. Robinson in *Machine Politics: a Study of Albany's O'Connells* points out, it speaks volumes that the O'Connells were so familiar with the Albany underworld that they could come up with the names.) The first list contained Oley's name. The kidnappers did not respond. Then came a second list, again, with no response. They knew it was only a matter of time before Manny Strewl, the name they wanted to see, popped up. On the third day, it did. The kidnappers concocted a letter to Strewl, sent from New York City, assigning him the task of go-between. "You no doubt are acquainted with the O'Connell people," it read. "Well you can be of great service to them. We have checked on you and decided to pick you as our go between *if you are willing*." In response, Strewl contacted—or at least pretended to contact—the kidnappers a half-dozen times, mostly in New York City and once in the saloon on the ground floor of the very building where John O'Connell was being held. The whole plan in its intricacy presaged the complex machinations that were to come in the famous Bath Beach armed car robbery in front of the Rubel Ice Company.

The authorities suppressed information about the crime for days and when the news became public, they put out the word that the O'Connells were not cooperating with the authorities. In fact, the family and police were working closely together.

Investigators quickly identified three suspects: Strewl, Oley, and Geary. They did this by figuring out which members of the Albany underworld had disappeared from their usual haunts.

A week after the kidnapping, Strewl met with Daniel O'Connell in Washington Park in Albany to talk about the ransom. They eventually settled on a payment of $42,500. O'Connell gave the cash to Strewl on July 28. Raising the funds had not been a problem; the county had offered the family as much money as they needed. A family member declined, reportedly saying, "Thanks a lot, but the money is coming in so fast we don't know what to do with it."

Strewl gave everything but his fee of $2,500 to the gang. The next day, he picked up O'Connell, drove him back to Albany, and delivered him to his uncle Dan. For 23 days, Butch had been blindfolded and chained to a bed.

After O'Connell was released, Strewl was questioned, but played dumb. He could give no solid description of any kidnapper or provide license plate numbers. Butch O'Connell was home safe, but his kidnappers had made off with the ransom and remained at large. Strewl, however, was not off the hook. Police eventually arrested him and charged him with the kidnapping. He was tried in March 1934, defended by "Legs" Diamond's lawyer. Experts declared that Strewl's handwriting was in letters between the kidnappers and the O'Connells.

Strewl was convicted and sentenced to fifty years in prison. An appeals court overturned the conviction, but he pleaded guilty to blackmail and received a fifteen-year sentence. The O'Connell family did not want to stop there. They wanted the men who were really behind the crime. They issued a "wanted" poster with pictures of the Oley brothers (Francis Oley, John's younger brother, was also involved), Geary, and the wives of the three men, and offered $15,000 in reward money for their capture.

In the complicated world of early twentieth-century big city machine politics, few thought the case was a straightforward trade of a powerful family's scion for cash. Other motives were tossed around.

Some suggested that Butch was abducted to settle his father's gambling debt.

Others theorized that the kidnapping was carried out to punish the O'Connells for failing to pay for a contract killing. The theory goes like this: "Legs" Diamond was angling to grab a share of the O'Connell family's bootlegging business before the end of Prohibition. To put a stop to that, the O'Connells hired someone to kill Diamond, promising a share in their Hedrick brewery as compensation. Under this theory, attributed by Frank S. Robinson to "a confidential source close to the kidnappers," the hired killer of Diamond never got their share of the brewery. The kidnapping was payback by that killer—who the author William Kennedy suggests may have been John Oley himself. If true, it casts a more sinister light on Oley. He would have been a murderer, not just a kidnapper and armed robber.

Kennedy mined this history for the second novel, *Billy Phelan's Greatest Game*, in his Albany trilogy that began with *Legs* and ended with *Ironweed*, giving Oley and Geary a measure of immortality they never would have expected. In the middle work, written in 1978, the O'Connells became the McCalls; John O'Connell the kidnap victim became Charlie Boy McCall, a "soft, likeable kid gone to early bloat, but nevertheless the most powerful young man in town, son of the man who controlled all the gambling, all of it, in the city of Albany, and nephew of the two politicians who ran the city itself, all of it, and Albany County, all of that too: Irish-American potentates of the night and the day." Strewl became Morrie Berman, "the son of a politically radical Jew, grandson of a superb old Sheridan Avenue tailor."

The novel centers on a journalist named Martin Daugherty, a pivot between the Albany demimonde inhabited by Billy

Phelan and the political class of the McCalls—who Kennedy describes as exercising a "stupendous omnipotence over both county and city, which vibrated power strings even to the White House." Phelan is a key figure who hovers on the edges of the kidnapping. As in real life, the Strewl character, Berman, chosen from a list of names in the newspaper, acts as a go-between. He receives a letter: "We got Charlie Boy and we want you to negotiate." Berman mediates the release of Charlie Boy, and the next day, an Albany hoodlum named Honey Curry is shot dead by police in Newark and another, named Hubert Maloy, is wounded. Ransom money is found in their pockets. Curry and Maloy seem likely stand-ins for Geary and Oley. The next big caper of these two real-life characters, in Bath Beach, could also be the stuff of fiction.

CHAPTER 4.

No. 330: Baking Powder: "Their Difficulties Are Well Known"

AS THE LIFE WAS DRAINING AWAY from Bennie the Bum at 334 Riverside Drive following the Rubel robbery, and as his confederates were dealing with his death and disposal, a middle-aged couple just four doors down was living in splendor in one of the great homes on Riverside Drive—a place filled with oak wainscoting, parquet floors, a delicate parade of plaster nymphs, garlands, rosettes, and slender torches on the walls. The house at 330 Riverside Drive was also stuffed with jewels, silver plate, and art, a source of booty far closer and more accessible than an armored car near the Brooklyn waterfront.

The contents of the home, occupied by George and Lucretia Jephson, are known in precise detail because of an insurance appraisal that survives from 1916. Thanks to the appraisal, meticulous restoration by the current owner, and the retention of original furniture, 330 Riverside Drive exists as a time capsule, a glimpse into the lives and trappings of the New York City gentry almost exactly a century ago. Guests at 330 stepped through the front door into an oval entryway with interior glass doors bowed outward to a small reception room. For all the grandeur of the exterior and the knowledge of the wealth that dwelt inside, a visitor would have found the entry area surprisingly small and cozy, a casualty of having to design a grand mansion in a townhouse footprint. A fire crackled in the inglenook—a small recessed fireplace with two small benches extending from each side. Maybe the polar bear skin rug had been brought up from the vast basement, where it shared space with trunks, saws, and carpets. In the reception hall dotted with plush silk cushions and oriental vases, visitors left their umbrellas in a rack and deposited visiting cards in a tray.

The billiard room with its full-size oak table, Austrian beer steins, and large leather cushion chairs was to the left, off the entry area. It still has a manly brick fireplace and glassed-in book cabinets. Off to the right was the room of the butler, Henry, who while employed there in the middle 1910s slept on a single-sized hair mattress on an enameled bed. Also to the right was a servants' sitting room, the pantry, and the kitchen with its thirty-four-piece aluminum cooking set, two coffee roasters, and rocking chair, where the cook rested after preparing the dinner and before climbing the stairs to her room on the fifth floor. (The benevolent visitor might have hoped that the Jephsons let the cook use the house's tiny elevator, a floating birdcage of narrow metal bars, antique button controls, and a sliding metal grate door. George Jephson probably made sure that was the case. He was a decent and kind man.)

The first floor also housed a sterling silver storage chest with service for twelve, which would have been laid out on the massive mahogany table in the dining room upstairs for dinner parties.

Climbing up to the second floor on the Georgian-style staircase, dinner guests trod on maroon carpet from Axminster, the posh British purveyor dating back to the eighteenth century. Here they arrived at the main area for public display: a grand reception room filled with vases and figurines, with another inglenook fireplace.

They then passed through a doorway topped by downward curving transoms that evoked the flowing lines of the Art Nouveau movement that was peaking at the time of the building's construction. Entering the drawing room, they would have been greeted by Lucretia and George. The room had a Baroque feel, all French empire curlicues and damask panels. Two Persian silk rugs seemed to float on the floor. Ivory carvings, Dresden figurines, and gilt candelabras adorned the tables and sat inside a lacquered bric-a-brac cabinet.

With dinner served, the guests passed through a door at the far end of the drawing room into the grand dining hall, squeezing past a hulking buffet table carved from Chilean mahogany and sporting floral motifs and carved grotesque faces as drawer pulls. Murals above the wood paneling stretched around the room and depicted woodland scenes (they are still there). The table, which had six extension leaves, marched down the rectangular room, surrounded by leather upholstered dining chairs made from the same Chilean mahogany. The Jephsons' two maids laid out the gold-embossed Limoges dinner set. Finger bowls, burgundy glasses, cut-glass water tumblers, and covered crystal fruit salad servers occupied each place setting. George sliced the roast with a buck horn carving set and at the end of the meal would have passed around the sterling silver nut dishes. Henry went to the butler's pantry off of the dining room to seek out any extra flatware or plate that was needed. The fresh-cut flowers from the tile-floored conservatory at the other end of the dining room added a dash of bright colors to the mahogany gloom.

Lucretia was an opera-lover—the family had a box at the old Metropolitan Opera house at 39th and Broadway, at a time when Toscanini was conducting there—and a singer herself. So after dinner, the guests probably glided back through the drawing room, went back out into the second-floor reception room, and passed into the music room on the other side, with its windows facing Riverside Drive. It held a Steinway Model C grand piano, two dozen chairs for an audience, and twenty-one volumes of music, along with 375 individual pieces. For guests with their own musical talents, there was a wood flute and a banjo. Lucretia may have plucked out a few arias from the shelf and sung in a fluty voice. The men likely politely withdrew to the library to smoke, and the women returned to the drawing room. Drawing from a cut-glass humidor, George and his male guests would light up and form groups to chat, to sit in the Flemish oak carved chairs, to examine a pair of Goerz field glasses or the bronze writing set sitting on an oak library table. Lucretia's family, the Davises, despite their origins in the wilds of upstate New York, were a cultured clan, or had pretensions of being so. On the bookshelves were multivolume collections of Shakespeare, Hawthorne, Hugo, Dickens, James Fenimore Cooper, Oliver Wendell Holmes, Poe, Longfellow, Tennyson, McCauley, and the memoirs of Ulysses S. Grant, who was entombed a mile to the north. Several hundred miscellaneous books also lined the shelves.

The guests saw the public rooms, but 330 Riverside extended upward three more floors. Lucretia's bedroom (listed as Mrs. Jephson's in the appraisal—with no reference to Mr. Jephson) was on the third floor. She slept in a four-poster canopy bed, part of a four-piece bedroom suite, and her belongings abounded in the chamber: items for the toilette, a gold miniature Louis XIV jewel case, crepe de chine and black poplin suits, silk lounging robes, opera glass bags, an ostrich feather collarette, and Japanese embroidered fans. The rear guest room on the third floor was filled with similar items of clothing and accessories. A fur wardrobe had scores of muffs, stoles, capes, coats and wraps with fur collars, and pillows.

The fourth floor had a half-dozen bedrooms and dressing rooms, which were filled with belongings and seem designed for storage, and a large cedar chest. The fifth floor had the maids' rooms, a linen closet, storage rooms, a wardrobe room, and storage room for the servants.

Lucretia amassed a large collection of jewelry. The appraisal lists a mountain of pins, necklaces, pendants, rings, chains, and bracelets, all valued at $25,941.25, or nearly $570,000 in today's dollars. The centerpiece? A diamond necklace with fifty-five stones, appraised at $9,000, worth about $200,000 today.

This opulence was made possible by a product that a super-market shopper to this day will usually find in the baking section, often nestled amid the sugar and cake mixes and yeast. Its label has remained familiar for more than a century: a red shield, gently curved at the bottom and the top, sitting on a bright orange background. On the shield are the words DAVIS, sagging down at each end; BAKING, running straight across; and POWDER, curving upward in a slight smile. The tiny letters "O.K." sit in a circle. It's a simple label for a simple product—a combination of bicarbonate of soda, acid salt, and cornstarch—a product that infuses baked goods with carbon dioxide so they rise, or leaven. On that, Robert Benson Davis built a fortune that provided the comfortable life for his daughter Lucretia and her husband. But it was a long and turbulent journey to arrive there.

Davis was born in 1843 in Pompey, New York, a town just outside of Syracuse. At sixteen he made the trek to New York

City and went to work for a wholesale grocer named J. Monroe Taylor. After the outbreak of the Civil War, the eighteen-year-old Davis was back in the town of Manlius, near Pompey, to enlist for a three-year term with the Union Army on August 15, 1862. (Listing his occupation as farmer, he was certified in the enlistment papers boilerplate as "entirely sober" by the recruiting officer; the new recruit signed his papers "R. B. Davis," and was called by those initials throughout his life.) Davis joined the 1st New York Mounted Rifles, assigned to Company L, a unit that drew on Syracuse-area men and was mustered in September. During the war, R. B. served in North Carolina and Virginia, where he took part in the battle at Spotsylvania Courthouse. He was discharged in Richmond, Virginia, on June 12, 1865, a twenty-two-year-old blue-eyed, five-foot-six-inch tall veteran with the rank of private. R. B.'s military records show he had been immediately promoted to corporal on enlistment, but something seems to have gone wrong because he was returned to private in May 1864. That didn't prevent President Lincoln from giving Davis a commendation at the White House.

Little is known about the next fifteen years or so in Davis's life, but he must have learned something about the dry goods business, manufacturing, and acquiring capital, enough to establish a baking powder producer in either 1878, 1879, or 1881, depending on which account you believe. He called it the R. B. Davis Company. The company's first location was at 112 Murray Street in lower Manhattan, after which it moved to 15 Hudson Street, then 90–92 West Broadway. In 1890, R. B. established a factory in Hoboken; the corporate offices joined it during World War I. The R. B. Davis Company also made cornstarch and cocomalt, a heavily advertised powdered chocolate drink, and distributed Cut-Rite Waxed Paper.

At thirty-eight, having just set up his business, Davis decided it was time to find a wife. On May 31, 1881, he married Jennie Weed nine days after her eighteenth birthday. Their only child, Lucretia, affectionately known as Lulu, was born four years later.

By the turn of the century, R. B. was a prosperous business-man, known as the Baking Powder King, with a much younger wife and a daughter in her twenties. In 1905, he joined the pioneering wealthy who saw a Riverside address as a sign of prestige, acquiring the most elaborate and Parisian of Farley's buildings, No. 330.

It was a beauty, but in one way an odd one. The facade on Riverside Drive is technically the public face of the building, the first in the row of townhouses. It is well proportioned, with each floor distinguished by a different style of windows, and with symmetrical variations within each row. The third floor has an elegant stone balcony topped with a broken pediment. But there is no entrance on Riverside Drive. The south side, on 105th, has the grand entryway and a long, grandiose canvas of architectural elements on what is essentially the side wall of a typically sized townhouse.

A large frame lined by small quoins (ornamental stone slabs) rises up to the top floor from the doorway, which is posi-tioned about three quarters of the way to the western end of the building and is topped by imposing brackets. The windows and balconies above the doorway vary in form from the rest of the facade. A large cartouche—that indispensable Beaux-Arts decorative oval surrounded by scrollwork and designed to dis-play a family's ancient coat of arms—crowns the frame above the fourth floor. (Needless to say, ancient coats of arms are not common on Upper West Side cartouches.) Horizontal cuts—called rustications in architecture-speak—score the limestone facade on the first floor, which presents a solid, almost fortress-like attitude. Quoining on the side walls reins in a frolic of ornamental brackets, balconies of metal and stone, carved acanthus leaves, and pediments on the front facade, which in the upper floors is faced with light tan brick.

To the right of the entryway is a facade punctuated by four bays. Grilles and metal balconies adorn the windows. A mansard roof bedecked with cartouches and arched dormers sits atop the building. A one-story conservatory separates No. 330 from the building to the east on 105th Street, with the space above the conservatory providing air and light for the stories above. It is the most detailed and high-quality work by Janes & Leo on the block, a showcase of Beaux-Arts technique. "This selective use of ornament underscores the care taken in every aspect of the design of a building such as this to create a coherent and dignified whole," the City Landmarks Preservation Commission said.

But whatever happiness R. B. managed to enjoy there evaporated within a few years. The home became a scene of scandal and discord.

In the fall of 1910, after nearly three decades of marriage, Davis sued his wife Jennie for divorce. The newspaper narratives cast Jennie as the villain. They portrayed her as a manipulative conniver and their marriage as a rancorous, even bizarre, union. Davis charged that Jennie tried to have him declared insane so she could seize his business, accusing her of telephoning executives of the company to say he was losing his mind. She intercepted his mail while keeping him trapped in his house under the surveillance of nurses. Was he insane? Not at all, retorted the old soldier. Just look at the success of his baking powder business.

Then there was the Harry problem.

According to an account in the *New York Times*, the Davis marriage "had been happy until his house became crowded with his wife's relatives. And he especially names Harry W. Weed," mistaking the middle initial. Harry H. Weed was the baby of the family, the last of seven children, thirteen years younger than his sister Jennie, and her pet. The clan came from Montour Falls, in upstate New York, seventy-five miles from R. B.'s birthplace of Pompey. It's probably true that Weed family members were frequent guests at 330 Riverside—at least they were after R. B. moved out, according to the family's letters. But Harry seems particularly to have gotten under R. B.'s skin. The divorce complaint said that while Davis was sick, "his wife would nag him and Weed irritate him into bursts of temper, which were further aggravated when Weed began taking stenographic notes of his language" to use as evidence of his insanity. The Weed siblings supposedly tried to force R. B. into a depression by showing him a doctor's report indicating that he had tuberculosis.

But the reference to Weed lingered and acquired a salacious cast. The implication was that Weed and his sister were just a little too close, more so than was healthy between siblings. The rumor has rankled the Weed family to this day. Harry's granddaughter, Brenda Steffon, dismissed the idea. "They were just siblings who held an affinity for each other," she said. "That relationship tainted R. B.," she said.

Back during the legal battle, R. B. sought to dramatize the extent of his abuse, twice recounting what he described as daring escapes from his own house. Once, he said he dropped a letter to a friend from a fourth-floor window, asking for help. The friend sent a car, and Davis said he slipped out when the servants were distracted by clearing his dinner dishes, and headed for another home he owned, in Summit, New Jersey. Then he engineered an escape from the Summit house, dressed as a doctor and accompanied by two nurses in uniform. His destination was Los Angeles, where he filed the divorce case. A year after filing, Davis backed away from his more corrosive charges, telling the court that his wife had merely grown tired of him.

Part of the dispute involved R. B.'s will. A letter introduced in court from Jennie, addressed to "Bob," complained that Davis's bequest would reduce the annual living allowance to Lucretia, who lived in the house, from $20,000 to $9,600. "Unless you change this, I shall be compelled to allow Lucretia to go on the stage, and you will be responsible if she falls into the many pitfalls of that career and becomes a low woman," Jennie Davis wrote. "It costs $40,000 a year to run the New York house. You must let us have more money after you are gone." The letter was reported in newspapers at the time but the writing style, and its salutation to "Bob," raise some suspicion. Neither matches original letters from Jennie that have survived. But more on these doubts in a moment.

The press introduced another element into the Davis battle: an affair between R. B. and his nurse, identified as "Miss Arthur." Referring to the Davises, the *Washington Post* said in a dispatch that "their difficulties are well known among their friends in the East." The article continued, "The friends have no hesitancy in declaring that the septuagenarian is eager for a divorce, so that he may marry Miss Arthur, his nurse." Certainly rumors about an affair between the two were circulating. R. B. asserted Jennie believed them. Privately, Jennie denied ever seeing Miss Arthur as a threat, calling R. B. "such a damned ass" for making the claim, according to a letter from Jennie to Harry several years later.

Jennie and Lucretia, who remained close, headed out to the coast for the legal case. They brought along their lawyer,

Delphin Delmas, who had recently been involved in one of the most sensational cases of the time: the murder of the architect Stanford White. Delmas had defended the man who killed him, the eccentric millionaire Harry K. Thaw. Thaw shot the architect out of jealousy for White's affair years earlier with Thaw's wife, the showgirl Evelyn Nesbit. The case notably introduced the public to Nesbit as the "girl in the Red Velvet Swing," a reference to an accessory in White's love nest. Delmas managed to win his client a verdict of not guilty by reason of insanity, even though Thaw had shot White in a crowded theater and cheerfully admitted it. Delmas scored a temporary victory for Jennie in Los Angeles when a judge ruled against R. B. on the grounds that he did not have legal residence in California.

Jennie filed her own motion for financial support pending the divorce, demanding a $5,000-a-month stipend—the equivalent of about $115,000 today. The judge, Walter Bordwell of Superior Court in Los Angeles, denied the request, saying she did not deserve the money because, he declared, she had temporarily driven Davis from his home in 1908 when he was sick. Another judge had already granted her $1,500 in a monthly living allowance, along with $1,500 for court costs and $10,000 for lawyers' fees. It appeared that the case had gone against Jennie, but she did not give up. She had Delmas launch an appeal.

Reports on the case were based mainly on Davis's testimony, his divorce complaint, and information that seemed to come from his side. But just how true was this portrayal of Jennie— the much younger wife—as the evil manipulator? It smacks all too much of the sexism of another era. How likely was it that Jennie would receive a sympathetic portrayal before courts and the court of public opinion when her husband was a powerful businessman? The narrative of a conniving younger woman seeking to steal the fortune of an ailing Civil War veteran may have seemed just too tempting to resist, whatever the truth may have been.

Letters from Jennie to Harry and from Harry's father to him around the same time, the period of 1914–1915, paint a very different picture. Jennie emerges as a bitter, wronged woman who felt abandoned after years of loving and taking care of an elderly husband, yet at the same time susceptible to any sign that R. B. might still care for her and want to help her financially. She was dogged by insecurities, about where she would end up living and how she would support herself. It's possible that Jennie connived just as the newspaper accounts had it. But it's likely we are getting an honest account of her feelings in letters to her brother Harry, the person she felt closest to in the world, aside from Lulu.

In the years after the divorce case, Jennie appeared to still be at 330 Riverside, but fretted over whether she had the "strength or heart to do what I have to in this big house." She also spent weeks at hotels in New Jersey, like the Monmouth Inn in Caldwell or the Hotel Montclair.

R. B. was unhappy too, it seemed. He had severe cataracts and feared going blind. "He said it made no difference one way or the other to him, for his life was wrecked anyway," Jennie wrote Harry. "He did not say who wrecked it," she added, an implicit assertion that it was not her. R. B. acquired a new house in 1915 but apparently not in his name, to avoid having to leave it to Jennie. "Harry, I don't think R. B. will do anything that is right by me again," she laments. Later she sees a photograph of the home. How strange it is, she writes, to see a picture of your husband's house.

R. B. stayed in hotels on visits to New York, and the couple found amicable moments. In May 1915, he visited 330

Riverside for dinner and spent several more evenings in his old home. When Jennie and Lucretia took him to the train station, presumably to head back to California, "he seemed to be glad to see me again," Jennie wrote. Even Harry was back in favor. Despite R. B.'s legal accusations against Harry, in private he considered him a "good-hearted fellow," Jennie wrote.

A calming force was on the scene by then: Lucretia's fiancé George Jephson, a solid, honorable Princeton graduate who was just establishing a business making auto bodies in Newark, New Jersey. R. B. thought highly of him, enough that he wanted George to immediately join the baking soda concern. But George declined to consider the matter until he and Lucretia were married—and only if she agreed. (They did, and she did.) George was solicitous of his future mother-in-law, and a frequent visitor.

But rancor over financial support continued, with R. B. refusing to give any further lump sums to Jennie, "for he did not want to do any more for the Weeds," Lucretia reported. "I hope he is going to stop and leave us all alone," Jennie told her brother, adding that her husband is "living to do what he can to injure his wife. But Harry I put all my trust on Jesus. He is *all* I have to turn to." Later she again frames her deep-set hurt in biblical terms. "R. B. does not write any more mean letters about any of us. I think it is time he stopped. *He has done all he can* to hurt us, but God is keeping him for something."

Her hatred for R. B. also infected relationships with her beloved daughter and steadfast son-in-law. Lulu's sympathy for her father got under Jennie's skin. "She thinks her father at times is all right and forgets all he has said and done to me, but she would not if he had done it to her," Jennie lamented to her brother. Two months after Lucretia and George married on September 8, 1915, Jennie complained how little Lulu asked about how she was doing or how little she offered to help, and declared her heart broken over what she interpreted as George's backtracking on an offer to have Jennie live with them. "He has said and done such mean things to me," she added.

A frequent refrain in her letters is her appeal in the divorce case. Over and over again she harps on it, and much of her life seems to revolve around the possibility of a ruling. "Harry I do not think what would happen to me if the appeal should go against me," she writes on March 14, 1915. Four and a half months later she expresses the same fear: "But I know I am *innocent*. Mr. Delmas says he has no fear but what I will be granted a new trial. R. B. says he will talk with me after the appeal is heard." Jennie goes so far as to tell Harry that if her daughter and son-in-law even dare to visit R. B. in California before the appeal comes, she will mark them as disloyal. There is an air of desperation about it all.

As the months pass, the appeal of the divorce case decision grows into an obsession. "Mr. Delmas just wrote me if his life depended on it, he should say it will be reversed, 'for you have both Law and Justice on your side. I never had a case that I felt more sure of,'" Jennie recounts in a letter of November 28, 1915, days before traveling to Santa Monica, California. "My appeal surely comes up in April court. I expect to be there if I am alive."

She never made it. Seventeen days later Jennie was dead.

Jennie bequeathed everything to her daughter, as did R. B. when he died five years later. Jephson had taken up his father-in-law's offer of a job with Davis Baking Powder, and on R. B.'s death assumed command of the company. The couple became the unquestioned master and mistress of 330 Riverside Drive.

Chapter 5.

The Planning, Stage 2: "One Good Ton Deserves Another"

THEY WERE WANTED BY THE POLICE upstate for the O'Connell kidnapping and hunted by Albany's political machine, but Oley and Geary operated openly in the New York metropolis. Stewart introduced them to Manning and McMahon, and they joined up as the Albany faction with the Manhattan West Siders. Naturally, Oley and Geary wanted to check out the armored car for themselves, so it was back out to Coney Island for another scouting trip to follow the vehicle. Oley asked if he could bring in his brother Francis.

The group met in a furnished apartment on the East Side and then in public spaces to avoid suspicion of gambling. Geary and the Oleys in particular could not afford to be picked up by the police on a routine matter. Sometimes they gathered in Riverside Park, sometimes six miles or so down in Stuyvesant Square.

The gang grew. Manning and McMahon brought in a car thief named Joseph Kress, a fellow Yanowsky faction associate, to acquire the getaway vehicles. Kress said he would store the cars he stole in a garage on Atlantic Avenue in Brooklyn that belonged to his uncle.

The Oleys and Geary continued making trips to Brooklyn to trail the armored car, and in the process learned that it made irregular stops but always appeared at a loading dock at the Rubel Ice Corp., at Bay 19th Street and Cropsey Avenue in Brooklyn's Bath Beach section—just three and a half blocks from a police station. The gang members noticed something else. The armored car doors opened twice at each stop: once to let the first of the three guards out, who entered the office with pistols drawn for a collection, and a second time to let out another guard who covered the men returning with the money.

Just as it is hard to remember what life was like before the invention of the radio, the TV, the telephone, and especially handheld, do-everything computers, it is difficult to conceive of the days before a giant box in your kitchen, plugged into an electrical outlet, kept your food cold and fresh twenty-four hours a day. Before the invention of the refrigerator, a vital industry flourished to provide blocks of ice to homes across the city, usually coupled with the sale of heating coal, because the two operations followed the same distribution routes. The combination represented a lovely joining of two basic human needs: keeping the body warm and keeping it fed. It was a competitive, rough-and-tumble trade, and one of its most successful practitioners was Samuel Rubel.

Rubel, who was born in the then-Russian city of Riga, emigrated to the United States about 1903 at the age of twenty-one. He found work hauling ice and coal in a horse-drawn wagon and selling the goods door to door in the Brooklyn neighborhood of East New York, working the north side of Watkins Street. It was tough, relentless labor. He would rein his horse to a stop in front of a building and haul the block of ice or bag of coal up the stoop. Rubel earned enough to become a supplier to other peddlers, and by 1907 had established the Independent Ice Company. He expanded into shipping coal to the city by train. "One good ton deserves another," became his catch phrase.

By 1913, Independent had become the Rubel Coal and Ice Company, which embarked on expansion by absorption. In the mid-1920s, the company won control of three other firms, including the Ice Service Corporation. By 1928, more than thirty ice companies had been consolidated into the Rubel monolith, which was worth $40 million, sold four million tons of coal and ice a year, and racked up nearly $100 million in annual sales.

Then, just before the stock market crash of 1929, Rubel decided to focus his business on ice, selling the coal part of his company for $17 million. Doubling down on ice with refrigerators around the corner may seem like ramping up typewriter production at the dawn of the computer. But coal itself was succumbing to a coal derivative, called coke, and oil.

Throughout the rise that made Samuel Rubel the king of ice and coal, he was dogged by charges of bribery and unfair business practices. He was sued by competitors and partners and investigated by prosecutors and court-appointed special referees. Rubel's lawyers constantly fought efforts to have him questioned in court cases. His methods were the classic targets of trust-busters.

Take the case of the Paramount Ice Corporation. Stockholders accused Rubel of bribing key directors of Paramount to make the Rubel company Paramount's lone customer and limiting production to 50,000 tons a year, or 25,000 tons less than Paramount was used to producing, thus guaranteeing any other supply would stay out of the hands of potential rivals. Another Rubel tactic involved trying to win over customers from rivals by undercutting prices and even giving away free ice.

The authorities took note of Rubel's expansion, and prosecutors indicted him for conspiring to run a competitor out of business. The case went nowhere, but a partner, Henry Senger, who had invested $4 million in Rubel's company, promptly sued for fraud, claiming that the ice baron kept him in the dark about how the investment was used and gave him no say in management. Rubel countered by noting that he paid Senger a tidy salary of $50,000 a year and tolerated his three sons on the payroll. The case was settled, with Senger receiving most of his investment back.

By the early 1930s, Rubel was worth more than $30 million. He owned a thirty-two-room mansion in Roslyn, Long Island, and a home at 106 Marlboro Road in Brooklyn. He had the kind of wealth that attracted attention, especially from people looking to make a buck. Among them was a plumber's assistant who did some work in the Brooklyn house. The worker, clearly no criminal genius, left a note demanding that Rubel deposit $10,000 at a cigar store or his wife and daughter would be killed. The man was arrested after an accomplice went to the cigar store and was welcomed by police officers.

Along with his homes, Samuel Rubel from Riga, who started with a horse cart in Brooklyn, had fifty coal and ice warehouses and offices in New York City—including one in Bath Beach that on a summer day in 1934 was to deliver $450 to an armored car that had caught the attention of criminals from Albany and Manhattan's Hudson River docklands.

The proximity of the Bath Beach warehouse to the waters of Gravesend Bay lit a bulb in the minds of the planners of the robbery, some of whom had lived much of their lives on the east bank of the Hudson River. And so the gang, as their planning grew ever more baroque, decided that the escape route would be across the water close by the site of the heist. Now they had to add to their escape fleet. McMahon knew a boat owner from the Manhattan waterfront named John Hughes, whose resume included ferrying bootleg liquor, and brought him to a meeting. The gang members told Hughes that they wanted to depart the scene from a dock close to the Rubel plant. Hughes promised to supply a lobster dory to ferry the loot and its procurers, and at another meeting suggested bringing his partner, Thomas Quinn, in on the deal. Quinn's great virtue was that he owned a speedboat.

The scheme then ratcheted into high gear. It was becoming a reality. Like actors populating a set, the men hung around the Rubel loading dock to make their faces familiar to employees and residents in the area. Manning bought a three-wheeled wooden push cart, donned an apron, and made regular purchases of ice from the Rubel warehouse, which he later dumped. There was no reason to bother selling ice when serious money was soon to be made. Here, habituation was becoming the mother of inattention.

Everyone did his part. McMahon provided machine guns, possibly supplied by Yanowsky, and Geary promised to bring sunglasses to conceal the robbers' faces. They staged trial runs. On August 14, the gang was ready to go. Each man assumed his place, checked his weapon, and scanned the street nervously. But one important piece was missing: Quinn and his speedboat were not there. He eventually showed up late, but the delay spooked the gang and they aborted the operation. It was likely the careful John Manning's decision. Geary had swooped in, the seasoned criminal, and Manning and McMahon had let him take the lead in planning the robbery. But Manning, with his steely calm, was the field general, the man on the ground calling the shots. "He had no great amount of brains, but he had no nerves either," Jack Alexander wrote in the *New Yorker*.

CHAPTER 6.

No. 331:
"Gentlemen Prefer Blondes"

BEFORE THE AGE OF MASS-PRODUCED CLOTHING and modern department stores, women usually made their own dresses or hired dressmakers. Patterns published in magazines served as templates for the designs, giving birth to the modern fashion magazine. William Ahnelt, a German immigrant, played no small role in making that happen. He invented and patented a system that numbered the pieces of an article of clothing in a pattern so it could be assembled more easily. And he had another good idea: displaying those patterns not just as free-floating blouses and dresses, but illustrating them on actual people. The idea seems elemental given the fashion publishing industry of our time, but Ahnelt was a spiritual forbear of today's glossy magazines like Vogue and Harper's Bazaar.

Ahnelt was born in Berlin around 1864, and as a youth desired to enter the Berlin Academy of Art. His father wanted him to take up a more practical line, so Ahnelt went to work as an apprentice to a women's clothing designer before emigrating to the United States in 1890 and finding work in the fashion industry. His idea of showing clothing illustrations on actual people caught on brilliantly, and by 1903, Ahnelt's American

Fashion Co. was producing fifteen magazines for the women's garment and tailoring trade and the fur business. Nor was this his only accomplishment. He established a school for fashion designers and was one of the first to bring the latest Paris fashions to the United States. In 1899, he founded the magazine *Pictorial Review*, which was the last addition to the Big Six— the most popular and enduring women's magazines founded in the second half of the nineteenth century—joining *Ladies' Home Journal, McCall's, Delineator, Women's Home Companion,* and *Good Housekeeping.* By the mid-1920s, Ahnelt's magazine, which grew from a pattern book into the most sophisticated and worldly of the six titles, had reached a circulation of more than 2.5 million—astonishing even by today's standards.

For a decade, starting in 1915, *Pictorial Review* serialized novels by such celebrated authors as Edith Wharton (*Age of Innocence*) and lesser-known writers like Kathleen Norris, Mary Roberts Rinehart, and Sir Gilbert Parker. Its core business, however, was the selling of patterns, through merchants and by direct mail, with Ahnelt's patented "cutting and construction" guides, based on the chic garments illustrated in the magazine.

"Style gave *Pictorial Review* Patterns their initial success; Style is maintaining that success to-day; and Style will preserve it in the future," crowed the company in a typical full-page ad in the *Washington Times* on June 4, 1922. "Every well-dressed woman craves smart Style, in a simple housedress as well as in an elaborate evening gown. This is why millions select *Pictorial Review* patterns." Other ads carried more provocative headlines, like "Does a woman love her husband less when children come?" Ahnelt's business grew to occupy a twelve-story building in the garment district, now 214 West 39th Street between 7th and 8th Avenues, a hive of fashion businesses that still bears the majestic lettering PICTORIAL REVIEW COMPANY on the facade.

Even before the magazine's circulation peaked, Ahnelt became one of the first owners of 331 Riverside Drive, which he bought in 1912. (The previous owner acquired it in the foreclosure proceedings that befell the original developer.)

Ahnelt also owned property in New Jersey, much like R. B. Davis. In Anhelt's case, it was a Tudor mansion with sixty-four rooms and a six-story tower in Deal Beach, New Jersey, which had been built by Daniel O'Day, a key member of John D. Rockefeller's brain trust at Standard Oil. It was Ahnelt's summer retreat and became his residence upon his retirement in 1934. It was a short-lived retirement home.

Shortly before dawn on June 24 of the following year, a maid named Fannie Trunetz was asleep, alone, in the empty cavernous house. The barking of a dog entered her consciousness and she jolted awake to find her room filled with smoke. Fire was quickly spreading through the Deal Beach mansion. Four fire companies responded, but they were helpless: there was no source of water. They had to lay 3,000 feet of hose from the nearby town of Allenhurst to acquire enough water pressure to fight the blaze. Soon the house, on its fifty-four-acre plot, was reduced to smoldering debris. Ahnelt lost $20,000 in silverware, rugs, paintings, and books, along with all of his personal and business records. An invaluable archive detailing the history of fashion magazines was lost.

The fashion magazine impresario owned the twenty-six-room No. 331 for little more than a half-dozen years. In 1918, it was sold to a "woman client" of a real estate firm, the *Times* reported, using a rather coy description. The client, it turned out, was the twenty-one-year-old mistress of the press baron and would-be movie mogul William Randolph Hearst, who naturally provided the funds to buy the house. Hearst lived with his wife Millie just a mile south, in the Clarendon, an apartment building on Riverside Drive at 86th Street. The family's elevated palazzo occupied the building's three top stories and featured a vast banquet hall, a ballroom with balconies on each end, a domed living room, a dining room on the roof, and a half-dozen suits of armor from Hearst's medieval collection.

Hearst, whose son described him as "sort of a Stage Door Johnny," met Marion Davies (originally Douras), when she appeared in the 1915 Irving Berlin revue *Stop! Look! Listen!* Hearst was fifty-two and had been married to Millie for twelve years, but he fell hard for the eighteen-year-old showgirl. Hearst bought 331 Riverside Drive for Marion as part of his campaign to turn the chorine into a star, mainly through his press empire and personal wealth. His newspapers relentlessly promoted Marion, to the extent that Hearst would kill an accidentally lukewarm review of one of her silent movies. Marion seemed to have unlimited expense accounts and showed no shyness about using them.

The Chief, as Hearst was known, spent a fortune, more than $1 million—$17 million in today's dollars—remodeling the house on Riverside Drive. The love nest became a palace. A marble fountain adorned with cupids was placed in Marion's sitting room. One room was transformed into a library, with wood paneling and calf-bound rare editions, although there is no evidence that Marion was much of a bookworm. She did tell a reporter for a fan magazine that she read plays and "things I think would film." As for the calf-bound books, "I-I'll r-read all of these when I'm an old w-woman," the reporter quoted her as saying, reproducing a stutter that Marion overcame on stage and in front of the camera.

Hearst also installed two of Marion's sisters, Rose and Reine, and her mother and a crew of servants in No. 331, and then proceeded to buy the house next door, No. 332, for Marion's father, Bernard. He gave each woman money to furnish their own rooms. If Marion was going to be his mistress, no matter how secret their relationship and how eager he was to avoid scandal, it was important to Hearst that her family have status. As part of the Douras family improvement project, Hearst arranged for Bernard, a none-too-successful Brooklyn lawyer who was an amiable companion to the Chief, to be appointed a municipal magistrate. Marion supposedly told friends that the building was to be used as an office for her father, although it was apparent that he lived there. Rose's husband, George Van Cleve, an executive of Hearst's movie-making arm, Cosmopolitan-International Pictures, also lived at No. 331 in the effort to elevate the entire middle-class Douras family to a place of greater prominence in society. Yet it is telling that the 1920 census lists Davies as head of the household, with the occupation of "motion picture actress."

The result was to surround Marion with a continuous retinue. She and her sisters liked to drink, and a biographer of the actress, Fred Lawrence Guiles, suggests the liquor delivery boys from Broadway made frequent visits to the houses. The Douras family excesses lead one to wonder what their next-door neighbors, the proper Jephsons, thought of the clan.

The Davies mansion figured in a scene described by Anita Loos, the author of *Gentlemen Prefer Blondes*, the satirical novel about a gold digger with Hollywood ambitions. Loos had lunch with Hearst and Davies at Marion's home up on 105th Street (aka No. 331), and later that evening dined with Hearst and his wife at their palatial apartment in the Clarendon. "And when I took my place beside W. R. at his wife's table," Loos wrote, "he observed, with a naughty twinkle, 'Well, young lady, we seem to be sitting next to each other in rather diverse locations, don't we?'"

Marion achieved film stardom during her years at 331 Riverside. In 1917, after a series of hit roles in shows, she began fielding offers for movies, the logical next step for chorus girls who had arrived. Just a few years earlier, the mother of her next-door neighbor, Lucretia Jephson, had warned her darling Lulu that she risked becoming a "low woman" if she were forced to pursue a stage career. Lucretia married respectably and inherited well, avoiding that dire fate. For Marion, that wasn't even an issue, although the moralists of the day might have taken a different position. The stage was her entree into the world of a wealthy businessman and then a stepping-stone to Hollywood. Her first film, *Runaway Romany*, came out at the end of 1917, the first of a series of formulaic films featuring her in roles as a distressed damsel or maiden pure of heart. Hearst did not finance the movie, but was impressed and decided to back Marion's film career.

In his biography, Guiles presents the full complexity of their relationship, which lasted thirty-five years. Hearst felt he had to spend on Marion and keep her accustomed to a gilded-cage standard of opulence as a way of countering the possibility of her having affairs with younger men. Davies depended on him to establish her as a star, but stuck by him—truly loved him—even when she had reached that status. Yet she felt trapped and unable to set herself free from Hearst's support. If she was never going to become Hearst's wife, she would take a film career instead. And Hearst might have felt that Millicent would accept his relationship with a film star, but not a simple chorus girl. In Guiles's view, the blanket of Hearst-provided publicity and money helped shape the undeserved view of Marion as a mediocre actress—a judgment solidified by the pitiful depiction of Susan Alexander, the vaguely Marion-like wife of Charles Foster Kane, modeled after Hearst, in Orson Welles's *Citizen Kane*. Welles too believed that Hearst's public relations campaign did not serve Davies well. In an introduction to Davies's recorded memories, *The Times We Had: Life with William Randolph Hearst*, Welles wrote: "That vast publicity machine was all too visible; and finally, instead of helping, it cast a shadow—a shadow of doubt. Could the star have existed without the machine? The question darkened an otherwise brilliant career."

Hearst took a keen interest in the screenplays, scenery, casting, and direction of Marion's movies, determined to make her not just a star but a screen diva. He pushed her into historical and romantic roles ill-suited to her natural talents as a carefree comedienne. She made eighteen movies through 1924 with titles like *Cecilia of the Pink Roses*, *Buried Treasure*, *Enchantment*, *Getting Mary Married*, and *The Young Diana*. One of her biggest successes came in late 1922: *When Knighthood Was in Flower*. Based on a hugely successful 1898 novel of that name, *Knighthood* was a big-budget, lavish historical epic about Mary Tudor, Henry VIII's sister, who is in love with a commoner despite her brother's demand that she marry Louis XII of France. The movie was a big hit, receiving positive reviews from newspapers, including those not owned by Hearst. Three decades later, Davies recalled the movie's opening night at the Criterion Theater. She had prepared a speech for afterward but the lights went up and the crowd left the theater before she had a chance to deliver it. She was glad of that, she said, despite having spent her dinner trying to memorize the words. Davies also remembered the long rehearsals of fencing scenes.

A play based on the novel had a hugely successful and lucrative run just twenty years earlier—starring, and directed by, none other than the actress Julia Marlowe, who owned the townhouse just a few doors down from Marion's home (see Chapter 14).

Hearst's other base of operations was in San Francisco, and he was busy in those years building the massive San Simeon castle retreat. Between that and the movie industry's gravitation away from New York and toward Hollywood, Marion was spending an increasing amount of time in California. Then a New York scandal made the move permanent.

William J. Fallon was a prominent "mouthpiece" of the day, a lawyer for gangsters who was also involved with two stock swindlers, Edward Fuller and William McGee. Their firm, Fuller & McGee, operated with impunity in defrauding investors, thanks in part to the protection of the Tammany Hall boss Big Tom Foley—a backer of Hearst's political nemesis, Al Smith. The swindlers, despite what appeared to be a strong case against them, managed to win acquittals at trial. The *New York American*, a Hearst paper, decided there was something fishy and assigned a crack reporter, Nat Ferber, to investigate. Ferber found evidence that Fallon had fixed the juries, and Hearst paid to put up witnesses in hotels so they wouldn't back away from their stories.

Fallon hit back, accusing the Hearst publishing empire of a vendetta against him (it was more likely that Hearst wanted to wound Foley, the Tammany boss). And he pulled out a would-be ace: he hinted he had some juicy information about Hearst and an actress. Fallon went on trial, dropped Marion Davies's name, and even intimated that he had birth certificates of her putative children. (The documents were never produced, Marion was not known to have had children, and historians doubt whether Marion ever became pregnant by the tycoon.)

The non-Hearst papers naturally went crazy over the story. To shield Marion, Hearst brought her out to California, eventually buying her a mansion in Beverly Hills.

In 1925, her upstanding Riverside Drive neighbors Lucretia and George Jephson (in No. 330) bought the Davies home (No. 331), differences in moral standards having no bearing on real estate. No. 332 was also sold and divided up into two- and three-room apartments. The Depression began taking its toll and by 1930, six families lived in No. 332, mostly immigrants with husbands working as rug merchants, salesmen, and teachers, and rents ranging from $100 to $150 a month. The trail of No. 332 peters out almost before it begins. Within several decades, it was demolished.

CHAPTER 7.

The Heist, Part I: "Ramshackle or Abandoned Mansions"

BROOKLYN'S BATH BEACH NEIGHBORHOOD LIES NORTH-WEST of Coney Island and its edge serves as the shoreline of Gravesend Bay, a pocket of water cupped to the south by thumb-shaped Coney Island and facing Staten Island's long shoreline slouching off to the southwest. The neighborhood is situated just below the Narrows, the spot where Brooklyn and Staten Island are closest, a gap now spanned by the Verrazano-Narrows Bridge and leading into Upper New York Bay. Just inland from Bath Beach was the heart of New Utrecht, which was founded in 1661 and was one of the six original towns that made up early Brooklyn. In 1776, British troops landed at the shore of Bath Beach on their way to the Battle of Brooklyn.

In the 1800s, Bath Beach served as an elegant resort, named after Bath, England, with acres of farmland. It was controlled by the Benson family (who gave their name to Bensonhurst). Another family of landholders, the Cropseys, who were descended from an eighteenth-century immigrant from

German-speaking lands, gave their name to the avenue that runs parallel to the bay shore and was near the Rubel factory.

By the 1930s the Bath Beach neighborhood featured a "cluster of small houses and ramshackle or abandoned mansions and hotels leading down to a deserted beach," according to the 1939 *WP'A Guide to New York City*. It is only twenty-four blocks long, cut through lengthwise by four main avenues: 86th Street is the boundary to the northeast, then Benson Avenue, Bath Avenue, Cropsey Avenue, and the Shore Parkway, which is now cut off from the water by the wide Belt Parkway.

On the morning of August 21, 1934, the block of Bay 19th Street between Bath and Cropsey Avenues murmured with an urban calm. Children watched tennis players thwack balls back and forth on a group of five courts on the south side of the street. Directly across, on the north side, was the Rubel Ice Company building, with an office and two sets of three loading bays. A few cars were parked nearby. Women sat on the stoops of several houses. Grass sprouted from cracks in the sidewalk near a fire hydrant. A moving truck driver, William McGee, sat in his cab. A muddy pothole occupied a piece of the street. A block and a half away, Gravesend Bay glistened in the sun.

After the aborted attempt a week earlier, the underworld actors were back in position.

Manning, swaddled in a long white apron, stood by a peddler's cart near the loading bays. The cart was a simple wooden affair, a crudely nailed together, open-topped rectangle with three spindly wheels. Every recent day Manning had placed his cart in the same spot—right in front of the Rubel company office and a few feet from the little flight of stairs leading up to the loading platform—seemingly there to collect a shipment of ice, so that bystanders would get used to his presence. He was so convincing that on this August morning a little boy tried to buy some ice from him. Out of nerves or natural orneriness, Manning cursed at the boy and chased him away.

Geary also posed as a peddler. Some accounts said he was leaning against the loading platform, although a witness later placed him by the tennis courts, where Stewart lounged in a dark green suit and white cap. Like Manning, Stewart had been showing up regularly in the area and idling about, also letting the neighborhood become accustomed to his presence. Francis Oley was some distance away, stationed by a warehouse, probably across the street not too far from the Rubel company. John Oley stood near the loading platform with a machine gun hidden in a cart under a piece of canvas.

The gang members had taken precautions to protect themselves. They had spread a substance called collodion on their fingertips to avoid leaving prints. Originally formulated to fix photographic prints, collodion acquired a new use, under the brand name Newskin, to close skin lacerations. The men also did not shave for several days, to make identification more difficult, and brought along white gloves to make doubly sure no fingerprints were left behind.

Meanwhile, Wallace and the boatmen Quinn and Hughes crossed the bay in their launches and waited at the end of Bay 35th Street, about a mile away.

McMahon, driving a blue Lincoln, and Kress, in a Nash (both stolen), staked out the route, waiting for the armored car to pass by.

This morning, the stops before Rubel were numerous, the last one being a Bank of Manhattan branch at 86th Street and 20th Avenue, about five minutes away. Three guards were on board. Joseph Allen drove. In the back of the truck were John Wilson and William Lilienthal, whose twin brother was a New York City police officer and whose other brother was a police detective. At 12:25 p.m., after three hours on the road, it rumbled up to the Rubel building, a squat, rolling strongbox with a white roof, fenders over the wheels, a shatterproof windshield, and a cargo of cash.

CHAPTER 8.

No. 333: The Canavans, Bellow, and the Duke

ONE OF NO. 333'S FIRST RESIDENTS was an elderly widow named Mary Thornton Donnell, a proper Baptist whose only child died in infancy. Mrs. Donnell bought the townhouse in 1903 and lived there a scant three years until her death in December of 1906. Her life passed without much notice, except for newspaper reports nine months before her death about a fire, the first of at least three major blazes to strike our Seven Beauties. The fire broke out in the second-floor laundry room, *The New York Times* reported, adding that "Maggie, a sturdy servant girl, carried Mrs. Donnell in her arms down to the first floor."

A dramatic story, yes. But digging a little deeper into the Donnell family background reminds us how a single spot in New York can evoke some of the central strands of the nation's history — slavery, the settlement of the West, and the growth of Wall Street.

Mary's father was the plantation owner and slaveholder Colonel John Thornton, and Mary herself owned five slaves in 1860, according to a local account of Clay County, Missouri. Much more is known about her illustrious husband of forty-four

years, Robert Donnell, a Riverside Drive resident only by association, but someone whose own history begins in the early
nineteenth century.

Donnell was born on December 13, 1816, in Greensboro,
North Carolina, the grandson of a Revolutionary War veteran.
After graduating from the University of North Carolina, he
headed west, to Missouri, settling in Rock House Prairie and
acquiring a junior partnership in a general store at the age of
twenty-one. So began Donnell's travels through various retail
businesses and later, wholesale firms. He landed in St. Joseph
in 1843, the year the city was officially founded. St. Joseph
would become a place people passed through—Easterners
moving west in search of riches by way of the California Gold
Rush and Pony Express Riders heading both east and west.
(One of the arrivals was Jesse James, who moved to St. Joseph
in 1881 and was shot dead in his house by an associate named
Robert Ford. The house is now a museum. You can see the
bullet hole.)

Donnell soon married Mary, who was fifteen years his junior,
and his fortunes improved even more when Missouri increased
the number of bank charters in the state. He grabbed one, founding a branch of the Bank of the State of Missouri with a partner;
Mary's brother, John C. Calhoun Thornton, served as the bank's
lawyer. Donnell went on to help finance the Hannibal and
St. Joseph Railroad, help build the city's First Baptist Church,
where he served as a deacon and oversaw the Sunday school,
and become a trustee of William Jewell College, located about
sixty miles away in Liberty, Missouri.

Donnell was typical of a new type of businessman in
mid-nineteenth-century Missouri, a class of men who "migrated
from a seaboard slave state to the western frontier, founded suc-
cessive and often simultaneous ventures requiring imagination

and a high tolerance for risk, and went through several career changes," wrote the economic historian Mark W. Geiger. "All were part of a self-selected kinship and social network, and had obvious 'people skills.' The most common career path was from farming to clerking, to opening a store, to the wholesale grocery or dry goods business, and finally into banking."

At the start of the Civil War, when Missourians were deeply divided over the issue of slavery in their border state, many of these bankers threw their financial support behind the Southern states. In this, too, Donnell was typical. Rebel troops took control of St. Joseph early in the war, and Donnell favored a system that reimbursed merchants for goods seized by the rebels, effectively financing the Confederate war effort. For taking this position, he was jailed and put on trial for treason. General Benjamin Loan, the pro-Union commander of the Western district of the Missouri State Militia, said no one among St. Joseph's rebels was "more potent for evil" than Donnell. In 1863, as a result of these attacks, Donnell was banished from Missouri.

He moved on to the goldfields in the Montana Territory. "The area was a friendly haven for Missouri's ex-Confederates," Geiger wrote. Donnell's brother-in-law, a former Confederate officer, joined him in Deer Lodge County, (coincidentally another refuge for Jesse James). At this point in his life, Donnell was forced to backtrack from his days as a prosperous banker, and he opened a grocery store with a fellow Missourian, William Tutt. "The store charged frontier prices," Geiger wrote, "three dollars for a dozen eggs when miners' wages were four dollars a month." Following the usual pattern, Donnell and his business associates established a bank, where they sold goods and gave loans in exchange for the collateral of shares in mines or for ore, which Donnell and his partners sent via railroad to Baltimore for smelting.

Then came a dramatic and unexplained shift in gears. Donnell decided to conquer the nation's financial capital. In 1870, at the age of fifty-four, he moved to New York, leaving a frontier town of two hundred for the country's biggest metropolis. Donnell eventually joined up with another brother-in-law, Leonidas Lawson, who was married to Mary's sister Theodosia, and George Simpson to create the banking firm of Donnell, Lawson & Simpson, which profited from the vast railway expansion of those years. The firm made especially good use of its Western connections, handling municipal bonds of western cities and investing in mining operations in Texas and New Mexico.

By 1880, the Donnells were living on Madison Avenue. Donnell retired in 1884 and died in 1892. What happened to his fortune is a puzzle because at Mary's death, her estate was valued at only $75,000. Her nephew William was named the executor and Mary had instructed him to invest $50,000 and assumed the money would double. She then provided that $100,000 go to William Jewell College in Missouri, to be used to establish and maintain a "historical library" called the Robert and Mary Donnell Library. Perhaps the stock market didn't cooperate, or William didn't fulfill his promise, or William Jewell College had other ideas; in any case there is no record of such a collection. Another $10,000 was put toward the commissioning of portraits of her and her husband by what were described as "first-class artists" to be given to her sister, Theodosia. Other sums went to servants and her nephews.

While Oley and Geary in Albany and McMahon and Manning in Manhattan were approaching adolescence, while the Davises' bitter division was coming to a head, and while William Ahnelt's magazines were teaching fashion to a generation of American women, another New Yorker and his large family installed themselves at 333 Riverside Drive: David Canavan, who dug holes for a living.

Any New Yorker with minimal powers of observation will be aware of the constant building that goes on in the city. After the razing of an empty structure comes the first major step in construction: chewing out the ground—or often rock in Manhattan's crust—to prepare for the foundation. That work quickly disappears. The foundation is laid, the building erected on top, and no one is the wiser about the work. In the early years of the twentieth century, one of the busiest and most expert excavation companies digging out foundations was Canavan Brothers, formed by the brothers David, John, and Maurice.

David bought No. 333 in 1910. With the Canavan business on West 56th Street and his home on West 105th Street, David Canavan became a firmly rooted West Sider. He was also politically connected, a necessity for a businessman who bid for public contracts. Canavan, a man of impressive girth with a thick brush mustache, was a member of the local Tammany Hall chapter, the Nameoki Club, which had its base a few blocks away at 233 West 100th Street and was known as the "little wigwam," in the tradition of borrowing Native American terminology for Tammany Hall trappings. He also belonged to the National Democratic Club, the Catholic Club, and the slightly waspier New York Athletic Club, which years later would be the scene of another crime by one of the Rubel robbers. Canavan even formed his own political association and named it after himself.

Poor David Canavan did not get to enjoy his spacious new home for long. He died of what the *Real Estate Record* called "neuritis" on September 21, 1914, as the first shots of the Great War were being fired an ocean away. He was forty-seven. Funeral services started at his home and continued at the Church of the Ascension, another recently built structure in the neighborhood, on 107th Street east of Broadway.

The building industry grieved. "To enumerate all the work performed by his company would be a recital of the City's growth and progress in real estate improvements in the last 25 years," the bulletin of the General Contractors Association wrote on David Canavan's death. In fact, Canavan Brothers did the dirty unseen work to build New York, and their presence is widespread in numerous structures. Think of David Canavan if you step into the lobbies of the Apthorp, Belnord, and San Remo apartment buildings, or the University Club, 23rd Street YMCA, and Ethical Culture School. He helped dig the foundation holes below.

David Canavan's seven children (four sons and three daughters) included Estelle, who married a doctor in 1926; May, who married around 1940; and Helen. He also had a hot-headed son, William. In 1927, when he was thirty-two, William was driving with a woman from Queens named Anna Sheridan on Riverside Terrace near 177th Street when he stopped to check his tires, news reports recounted. At that moment, he later told police, two men he had never seen before stepped into the road. In a time-honored macho ritual, one of the men said something William considered insulting. He took a swing, and the loudmouth pulled out a gun and fired. Canavan was wounded in the leg, and the two men disappeared. The bleeding victim rode around in a police cruiser in search of the assailants, but to no avail. The *Times* quoted him as saying, "I could have gone to my private physician and you would have known nothing at all, but I was determined that if the police could catch these men I would see to it that they were punished." The origins of the shooting remained murky: one of his sisters was quoted as saying that the young Canavan was shot when he refused to put up his hands during a robbery. Whatever the circumstances, finding oneself shot was not considered the right sort of behavior by the Canavans' tonier neighbors.

Through the 1930s and early 1940s, 333 Riverside Drive remained in the Canavan family. In 1945, the grandson and namesake of David Canavan sold the building to an out-of-town investor and it was broken up into apartments. The following decade, Saul Bellow, then a forty-year-old literary transplant from Chicago, lived in one of them when he was writing *Seize the Day*, a novella about an unemployed, divorced, self-doubting salesman named Tommy Wilhelm.

In the novel, Wilhelm lives in an Upper West Side residence hotel called the Gloriana, and the book is studded with mentions of the neighborhood, including this particularly evocative passage:

> Along Broadway in the Seventies, Eighties and Nineties, a great part of New York's vast population of old men and women lives. Unless the weather is too cold or wet they fill the benches about the tiny railed parks and along the subway gratings from Verdi Square to Columbia University, they crowd the shops and cafeterias, the dime stores, the tearooms, the bakeries, the beauty parlors, the reading rooms and club rooms.

Wilhelm's father lives in the same hotel as his son, and a major theme of the novella is the old man's disapproval of his son's bad habits, grooming, and lack of achievement. Wilhelm, in turn, rails against his father's coldness and lack of sympathy.

The novelistic relationship is poignant, given Bellow's life at the time. In May 1955, his father died, and Bellow wrote the next month to the critic Leslie Fiedler from his apartment at 333 Riverside Drive: "Since my father's death last month I've been slow at everything. Not that I was ever prompt in anything, but life is particularly difficult in all departments right now."

Some years before Bellow sent his letter, 333 Riverside Drive had passed into the hands of another American cultural giant: Duke Ellington. The block became something of an outpost for Ellington's circle. In the late 1940s, the Duke had bought No. 334, and his sister Ruth Ellington James was living there with her husband Daniel James and young sons Stephen and Michael in a duplex on the top two floors. When No. 333 came up for sale, Ellington bought that one too. The owner wanted out, Stephen James recalled in an interview, after getting mugged in his own lobby. The two buildings became a thriving locus of the Ellington world. No. 333 housed the offices of Tempo Music, Ellington's publishing company, which Ruth ran, and included a room filled with awards and other Ellingtonia. Several other family members and friends lived in apartments in the two townhouses at various times, including Bernice Wiggins, Ellington's cousin, who had a place at No. 333 as late as 1980. Mildred Dixon, a former companion of the jazz great, worked for Tempo and lived on the ground floor of No. 334. No. 333 was also the scene of Sunday jazz salons and concerts, including a 1976 performance by Bea Benjamin, a South African protégé of Ellington's, with Johnny Hodges playing alto saxophone and Buster Williams playing bass. Ellington was said to have written songs there, and copyists used the office to produce musical scores of his compositions.

Ellington family members have incisive memories of the houses. In an interview shortly before he died in 2007,

Ruth's son Michael James recalled the glorious view and the mahogany-paneled living room at 333 Riverside Drive, and a birthday party for Duke, where he saw such luminaries as Joe Lewis, Sugar Ray Robinson, Ezzard Charles, Adam Clayton Powell, and Roy Wilkins. Also present was Louie Bellson, the Duke's drummer. "He spent the whole party hanging out with me because Louie didn't drink or smoke," James recalled. "He was just there to pay tribute to Duke on his birthday. He was a very dedicated musician. He was all about the drums. He spent the whole party showing me different drum patterns."

Mercedes Ellington, a daughter of Ellington's son, Mercer, who lived with her maternal grandmother, remembered visits to her Aunt Ruth at No. 334 and sunning herself on the balcony there. She spoke ruefully of a melancholy Sweet 16 party thrown for her by Ruth in the mid-1950s. Many invited guests failed to show. Others stopped by just to gawk at the house. "People came and went, and mostly went," she said. Stephen James recalled the front-room library at 334, mentioned Edward R. Murrow's 1957 interview with Ellington in the family apartment, and spoke of playdates with the daughter of Leonard Feather, the jazz writer and musician, who lived half a block up Riverside Drive in No. 340 and formed a record company with Mercer. He also mentioned the neighborhood's increasing seediness.

The James family moved briefly into No. 333 and left the neighborhood in the early 1960s, Stephen James said. Ellington bestowed No. 333 on Ruth, and gave the title of No. 334 to Mercer, who sold his building in 1975. Ruth sold hers in 1980.

Three years after Ellington's death in 1974, the city granted a new name to the street around the corner, West 106th Street, my street. It became formally known as Duke Ellington Boulevard, the result of a compromise between the Duke

Ellington Society, which wanted a street-naming closer to Lincoln Center, and the city, which the society said preferred a small street in Harlem. The law establishing the name-change made note of the presence around the corner of the "Duke Ellington Mansion," and though Duke is often said to have lived in 333 Riverside Drive, his survivors dispute the notion. "He never spent one night there," Stephen James said. But his spirit is indelibly present.

CHAPTER 9

The Heist, Part II: "Say a Word, and It Spits"

A S THE ARMORED CAR PULLED UP in front of the low-slung warehouse in Bath Beach, four trucks were lined up along the loading platform, waiting for ice deliveries. Because of Manning's cart, the armored car was forced to pull up about twelve feet past the entrance. The collection from Rubel that day was to be about $450. Following company protocol, the first guard, William Lilienthal, stepped out of the back of the armored car to head inside for the pickup. He shut the van door, his hand resting on the butt of his revolver. Next, John Wilson emerged from the car, prepared to cover Lilienthal. The green-suited Stewart, the connector of the gang's Albany and Manhattan crews, began moving stealthily toward Lilienthal from across the street. The peddler in the white apron—Manning—appeared to be rearranging burlap sacks on his cart but was actually digging out his machine gun.

As Wilson stepped onto the pavement from the armored car, Manning pulled out his gun from under the burlap sacks, aimed the barrel at him, and ordered him to raise his hands. "Say a word and it spits," Manning barked at the guard. At least, that was the quote provided by the newspapers, the kind of West Side gangster-speak that smacks of Jimmy Cagney. The reality of the situation did not immediately register with Lilienthal, who later said he thought it was a joke. "Come on, don't bother me. I've got no time for fooling," he said, according to what his wife Anna later told the *Brooklyn Eagle*. But Lilienthal became a believer when his eyes registered the gun.

Manning ordered Joseph Allen, the driver and third member of the three-man guard crew, out of the truck. Geary, who was close by, moved toward the group, followed by Oley, who kept his eyes on the end of the street. Allen later said he tried to sneak a look at the robbers but was discouraged with the words, "If you look around again I'll blow your brains out." That quote, at least, has the air of verisimilitude.

Geary veered over to close in on Lilienthal behind the truck, stuck a pistol in his back, and guided him into the Rubel office as Stewart went to the edge of the loading platform, which was as high as a man's stomach and ran along the facade for about eighty feet. Rounding up eight adults and several children standing nearby, Stewart forced them into the company's office. The other two guards and William McGee, the moving truck driver who had been waiting in the truck's cab, were ordered to huddle under the loading platform. Shut up, Stewart told the rounded-up adults, and all will be well. He then went into the office to back up Geary, who was there with Lilienthal.

Inside the office, Geary had forced Lilienthal onto the floor. Taking command as the more experienced executor of big-time crimes, he told Stewart to keep an eye on the guard. When Lilienthal raised his head and looked up, Stewart showed Geary his toughness, issuing a warning: do it again, and I will kill you. Stewart went over to rip a telephone off the wall. Outside, Francis Oley trained his gun on bystanders and kept watch on the people under the loading dock.

At that point, Kress and McMahon, who had been following the truck, pulled their cars up next to the armored car, Kress in the Nash and McMahon in the Lincoln. John Oley jumped into the back of the armored car and began heaving out bags of money and tossing them to Kress, Manning, and McMahon. The bags—about ten in all—were filled with bills in denominations of $20 and less. The back seat of the Lincoln had been removed to accommodate the loot.

The haul was $427,950, a not unusually large sum. William Dempsey, a vice president of the United States Trucking Corporation, later said that Tuesdays were the busiest days of the week and it was not uncommon for the armored car on the Rubel route to carry anywhere from $300,000 to $500,000. (This was the era before Internet banking and wire transfers, when large sums of cash routinely traversed the nation's streets and highways.) Although this was half what the gang was hoping to score, $427,950 amounted to the largest sum of money stolen from an armored car in the nation's history up to then. It would have been greater if the gang had not left behind $29,000 in heavy-to-carry coins.

Reporters quickly pieced together what had happened based on accounts from witnesses. William Kelly, a caretaker of the tennis courts and a military veteran, was on the street working on the car belonging to Carolyn Bannister, the teaching pro who owned the tennis establishment. Kelly astutely observed what was happening and quietly made his way to the courts, warned the players that a holdup was underway, and told them to lie down. The players took a while to believe him, but eventually did.

"I looked out and saw an armored car coming down the street," Kelly said. "The man with the pushcart wheeled the cart out in front of it while the man nearby ran up and got out the machine gun. I knew something was wrong then and gave the warning about stray shots."

Bannister, who was playing on Court 1, told the *Eagle*, "A man with a pushcart appeared shortly after I started and watched the game, looking through the wire screen. I thought it funny a pushcart man should be so interested in tennis, but I never guessed he had a machine gun hidden in the cart. At 11 o'clock," she continued, "I moved to an inside court and at 1 o'clock, just before 1 it was, one of the men employed here ran in and said: 'Everybody down, down on the ground: there's a holdup.' There were about eight of us on the courts, and we all dropped without knowing what was happening. Then there was a roar of autos down the street and we learned the details."

After the armored car was lightened of its load, John Oley climbed out and jumped into the Lincoln, where he was quickly joined by his brother and Geary. Kress got back in behind the wheel. Then McMahon took the driver's seat of the Nash with Stewart inside while Manning kept his gun trained on the people lying under the loading platform.

Manning then backpedaled toward the Nash. Just as Manning was climbing in, McMahon, at the wheel, released the clutch too quickly. The car leaped forward before Manning had gotten all the way inside, causing him to drop his Tommy gun in the street. After he tumbled in, the two crews tore off, with the cars rounding the right turn onto Cropsey Avenue off of Bay 19th on two wheels. In a bit of daring, Lilienthal picked up Manning's machine gun and jumped into the armored truck with his colleagues. They gave chase, spraying bullets at the getaway cars.

The Lincoln, license plate 1-L-5075, zoomed through the next cross street, 18th Avenue, and past a playground of the Children's Aid Society, which was crowded with youngsters. The potential for tragedy was great here, as a team of private security guards raced after the fleeing gangsters, firing wildly while children played nearby. The children were unaware of the danger; some said later that the shooting sounded like cars backfiring. Lilienthal fired seven more rounds as the Lincoln shot through the next cross street, Bay 17th Street.

The guards gave up the chase and the Lincoln doubled back to head south again and arrived at the water's edge, at Bay 35th Street, sixteen blocks away from the robbery site. Wallace and Quinn were standing by on a twenty-six-foot white Sea Bright dory, the *Popeye*, fitted out as a lobster boat. Its bow was pointed and its stern square, with an open cabin behind a windshield and a broken-off boarding ladder on the right side.

Hughes was manning a twenty-eight-foot mahogany-sided Gar Wood speedboat. When the men in the Lincoln arrived, they loaded the bags of money, labeled PUBLIC NATIONAL BANK and BROOKLYN-MANHATTAN TRANSIT COMPANY, onto the speedboat as John Oley, Manning, McMahon, and Stewart scrambled aboard. Hughes handled the tiller and Oley and Stewart sat along the sides as if they were out for an afternoon's pleasure cruise. Francis Oley, Geary, Wallace, and Kress jumped onto the lobster boat with Quinn at the helm. If approached, they planned to say they were out for a fishing expedition. A supply of fishing tackle would help give credence to their story.

CHAPTER 10.

No. 334: Adrenaline and "Sakura, Sakura"

O N THE COOL SUNDAY MORNING OF April 28, 1912, while David Canavan the contractor was probably taking his breakfast in 333 Riverside Drive and William Ahnelt, the magazine publisher who lived in No. 331, might have been looking over layouts or pondering his circulation, a compact man with a white mustache, its tips elegantly waxed upward, walked down the steps from the entrance to 334 Riverside Drive. (Twenty-five years later, members of the Rubel gang would haul their wounded comrade up those same steps.) The man was Jokichi Takamine, a Japanese scientist who spoke English with a combination of Scottish burr and Dutch gutturals, a sober, highly contained man who had isolated the hormone that causes less-controlled humans to panic and flee. The discovery helped make him the fortune that led to No. 334's purchase.

Takamine was also a major figure in the Japanese community in the United States. He helped bring about Japan's donation of thousands of cherry trees to Washington, DC, and, closer to home, was a member of a committee of Japanese residents who donated cherry trees to New York City. The trees were planted in Sakura Park, a two-acre rectangle named after the Japanese word for cherry blossom just north of Riverside Church, bordered by Riverside Drive and Claremont Avenue, and less than a mile up Riverside Drive from Takamine's townhouse. The gift came in conjunction with the Hudson-Fulton celebration of 1909, which commemorated the 300th anniversary of Henry Hudson's discovery of the river that bears his name. But the first shipment of trees destined for the park was lost at sea and a replacement had to be sent. So only now, three years later, was Takamine on his way to a dedication ceremony.

Some 5,000 people were on hand for the event. Thirteen little girls wearing flowery kimonos planted the last thirteen of the trees and performed a Japanese dance. An orchestra played excerpts from *The Mikado* (at the time, sadly, one of the principal representations of Japanese culture in the West), patriotic airs, the Japanese national anthem, and the cherry tree anthem—"Sakura, Sakura." Takamine delivered the main address, in which he thanked the United States for bringing to Japan "the seeds of Occidental civilization." He was carrying out a self-imposed mission of bringing the Japanese and Americans closer together.

"Those seeds have taken root in fertile soil and have brought forth a harvest, which is today the wonder and admiration of the world," Takamine said, according to an account of the festivities in the *New York Times*. "We people of Japan are not ungrateful. We do not forget what we owe to this wonderful young republic. Our affection for this country is deep-rooted, and has increased with every step of our national development, as, let us hope, the roots of these trees will with each passing year take deeper root in your American soil." Takamine pulled a rope, and the American and Japanese flags fell away from a commemorative tablet (since lost).

The Japanese consul general, Yasutaro Numano, delivered the final speech. He spoke of the reservoir of goodwill between the two countries and added what in retrospect seems an ominous note: "If the occasional voice of an alarmist is heard proclaiming the danger of war between the two countries, I think we have all learned that it is the voice of a demagogue or man speaking from selfish and ulterior motives. Like the Americans, the Japanese are a peace-loving people. That our friendship may never be doubted or our interests conflict I am sure is the devout wish of us all." (Fun fact: Sakura Park is also home to a statue of General Daniel Butterfield, a Civil War figure from the family that founded American Express and who is best remembered for composing "Taps.")

Takamine was essentially one of the world's first biotech entrepreneurs and a contributor to the vigor of the American economy at the beginning of the twentieth century. The inventiveness, commercial drive, and energy that fed America's economic rise was strongly driven by European immigrants. But Takamine is an example of the lesser-known contributions of Asians, and while his remarkable story is obscure in the United States, he is celebrated in scientific and business circles in Japan. One of the brightest young minds of his generation, he was singled out by the Japanese imperial government to help put the nation on the industrial map, ended up bringing his discoveries to the United States at a time of rising anti-Japanese sentiment, built major businesses, and became an important figure in the earliest years of relations between the two countries.

Takamine was born in Takaoka, a small town on Japan's western coast in 1854, the year that Commodore Perry and his armed squadron crowbarred Japan into opening trade with the west. His mother's family owned a sake brewery and his father was a doctor. Within a year, the family moved to the nearby town of Kanazawa, known for its sixteenth-century castle. Jokichi was a precocious little boy, and such boys were often sent to study in Nagasaki, one of the few Japanese cities with Western contacts. So at twelve, a tender age for such a long journey, he embarked for the distant city to study science, learning English from a Dutch family (which forced him to work as a houseboy). As a result, he spoke English with a Dutch accent for the rest of his life.

Jokichi went on to medical school in Osaka four years later, but after discovering a love for chemistry, he abandoned the course and entered the Imperial College of Engineering in Tokyo, where he studied chemical engineering on a government scholarship.

Japan in those years was intent on harnessing Western technology in the making of its own products, and Takamine was one of the chosen, a rising talent in science deemed worthy of absorbing knowledge abroad. So he was sent to study technology at the University of Glasgow in Scotland (where he picked up his slight Scottish burr). His specialty there was the manufacturing process for fertilizer.

The government brought Takamine back to work for the nation's Ministry of Agriculture and Commerce. But the man was too valuable to be stuck in a bureaucracy. In 1884, Takamine found himself in New Orleans, sent by the imperial authorities to take the post of co-commissioner at the yearlong Cotton Exposition. He took lodging at a large, dilapidated boardinghouse in the French quarter run by the strong-willed Mary Hitch, the wife of a Union officer who passed through New Orleans during the Civil War. The Hitches had five daughters; Takamine began courting the eldest, sixteen-year-old Caroline—twelve years his junior—teaching her tea-making ceremonies and the Japanese national anthem. They became engaged, with Mary's approval, despite the rarity of an American-Japanese match in the 1880s. The couple became fodder for the newspapers. It was a bold move for a young woman in the South, given the few Japanese nationals in the United States at the time and the often ugly stereotypes projected on them.

At the Cotton Exhibition, Takamine became intrigued by the use of phosphates as fertilizer, and he returned to Japan to test them out—as well as break the news of his engagement to his family. The phosphates tests were successful; the marriage announcement less so. The family was not happy with such an untraditional marriage, for it was viewed as inevitably harmful to Jokichi's social standing and business prospects.

Takamine remained in Japan for several years, establishing the Tokyo Artificial Fertilizer Company based on the phosphate experiments and also serving with the Bureau of Patents and Trademarks—good experience for his industrial future. He returned to New Orleans and married Caroline on August 10, 1887.

For the hard-working scientist, a honeymoon did not mean a European tour or jaunt to Newport, but a visit to South Carolina to investigate fertilizer plants and to Washington to study patent law. Caroline must have been a devoted wife to take the grand fertilizer tour. Eventually, the couple made it to California to embark for Japan and their lives as a young industrialist couple. They began a family: Jokichi Jr. was born in 1888 and Eben in 1889.

While working at the fertilizer company, Takamine had a sideline: developing an enzyme that would break down starch into sugar, a necessary step before fermentation. These enzymes were called diastases (later, amylases). The starches involved were corn, rice, and wheat, the raw stuff of alcoholic drinks, and Takamine's diastase could cut the fermentation time for grain alcohol from six months to forty-eight hours. He proudly called his enzyme takadiastase. It was the enzyme in rice mold, known scientifically as *aspergillum oryzae*, or *koji* in Japanese, and had uses in making soy sauce, miso, and sake.

Despite Jokichi's scientific success, life was not happy for the Takamines in Japan. Caroline was isolated, unable to speak the language, lonely, and unwelcome, facing downright hostility from her mother-in-law. The cold, the lack of privacy, the primitive plumbing, and the pervasive odor of fertilizer all afflicted her.

Takamine fared better with his mother-in-law, Mary Hitch. They corresponded frequently, often discussing business matters. She had taken an active role in promoting his work in the United States and had loaned him money. In 1890 she sent a telegram: a whiskey distillery in Chicago was interested in his enzyme. The enterprising Mary even established a firm called the Takamine Ferment Company, installing herself as president.

So the Takamines moved to the United States to make their fortune. He set up a factory in Peoria and began marketing takadiastase to the American beer and distillery industry as a faster, cheaper, and more productive agent than malt, which was commonly used in the West to break down starches before fermentation. Just as the American Caroline was ostracized in Japan, Takamine's Japanese origins did not endear him to the distillers. Nor was he a favorite of the companies that made malt, which takadiastase threatened to replace. The whiskey distillery where his process was being applied, on the verge of production, burned in a mysterious fire, leading to financial disaster. Takamine began suffering from hepatitis and his health declined precipitously.

However, he recovered both physically and financially and applied for an American patent for his process to make taka-diastase—the first application in the United States for a microbial enzyme. With the help of young scientists he brought over from Japan, Takamine discovered that the enzyme would be much more profitable as a treatment for dyspepsia because of its ability to catalyze the breakdown of starch in the stomach. Takamine persuaded Parke-Davis, a Detroit-based pharmaceutical company, to license it as a product. It was one of the company's early big hits, and for the first time, this government-groomed Japanese scientist's work was proving to be highly profitable. Products soon followed, with names like "Dr. Takamine's Taka-Diastase" on the packaging. Parke-Davis took him on as a consultant.

Takamine moved on to another project for Parke-Davis: attempting to isolate the active substance in the adrenal glands of sheep, which were in plentiful supply at the nearby Chicago stockyards. Scientists at the time had discovered that adrenal gland secretions could pump up the blood pressure in lab animals. Takamine moved to New York in 1897, where he set up his own lab in a basement on East 103rd Street to work on isolating the activating substance. Somewhat abruptly, he removed his mother-in-law from the leadership of the company and took over himself, deciding that a burgeoning international company could not be led by a woman. Mary died a few months later.

Soon Takamine's scientific work would lead to a greater success—indeed a landmark discovery in the annals of science. But accusations of intellectual theft and stealing credit would cloud his triumph.

As he pursued the adrenaline research, Takamine paid a visit to the lab of John Abel, a distinguished scientist at Johns

Hopkins University, where Abel had been working on a similar project. He brought some of Abel's methods home with him.

Among the young Japanese scientists Takamine employed in his Upper East Side lab was a twenty-three-year-old chemist named Keizo Uenaka. Uenaka worked long hours on the adrenal gland project, often falling asleep in the lab. Results were elusive. On a hot June night in 1900, he went home exhausted, without washing out the equipment. The next morning, he noticed crystals had formed in an unwashed test tube. It turned out to be an isolated form of adrenaline. Takamine, as director of the laboratory, quickly filed a patent and published several scientific papers under his name—without Uenaka's. He also trademarked the substance.

Uenaka's feelings are unrecorded, but his daughter expressed bitterness that her father did not receive more recognition. In any case, Uenaka swallowed any resentment of his own and worked loyally for Takamine for another sixteen years before finally returning to Japan and joining a company that Takamine had set up there. Uenaka eventually received some credit in 1966 when a journal sponsored by the National Museum of Science in Tokyo attributed adrenaline's isolation to the assistant.

As for John Abel, he felt "scooped and duped," in the words of Dr. Joan W. Bennett, a microbiologist who is probably the foremost scientific expert on Takamine's work. Abel had produced what he thought was a crystalline version of adrenaline before Takamine, although it later turned out to be impure. He argued that Takamine's crystals were also not unadulterated adrenaline—and he turned out to be right, although the state of chemistry at the time could not make that determination.

Abel did not challenge Takamine's patent, but a rival drug company argued that a natural substance could not be protected by a patent. It remains a fraught question, but in 1911 Judge Learned Hand ruled in favor of Takamine's claim, producing a quote famous in biotech patent circles: "I cannot stop without calling attention to the extraordinary condition of the law which makes it possible for a man without a knowledge of even the rudiments of chemistry to pass upon such questions as these."

Adrenaline—later also called epinephrine—quickly found medical applications, saving lives in cases of severe allergic reaction, cardiac arrest, and breathing emergencies. It became a key way for surgeons to control hemorrhaging. "The drug transformed surgery," Bennett wrote in an American Chemical Society article.

When a bee stings someone allergic to them, and an EpiPen saves that person's life, thanks can go to the good Japanese entrepreneur, although EpiPens generally have the synthetic form of adrenaline. The natural kind courses through our bodies when we are pumped up by fear or excitement caused by events like armored car robberies in Brooklyn.

Takamine was on the road to becoming a tycoon. He founded a laboratory in Clifton, New Jersey, calling it the International Takamine Ferment Company, and established the Sankyo Pharmaceutical Company of Tokyo to sell takadiastase in Japan, which lives on today as the multinational corporation Daiichi-Sankyo.

Takamine, at the time called "a well-known Japanese chemist of this city" by the *Tribune*, joined the life of the Seven Beauties in 1909, when he and his wife Caroline moved down from 45 Hamilton Terrace (near a lab of his on 142nd Street) and bought 334 Riverside for $85,000. They spent a fortune remodeling the place using Japanese motifs. Decor included panels depicting festivals, carved teak furniture, a huge hand-made bronze temple lamp, an inlaid dining table, and gilded grillwork on the walls. Thick carpets covered the floors and bouquets of violets rested on tables.

On one side of the newcomers was the wealthy Davis family in 330, with their disintegrating marriage and single adult daughter, and Ahnelt in 331, the fashion magazine king. On the other was the family of the industrious Lothar Faber, of the pencil-making dynasty, in No. 335.

The Takamines, with their sons Jo and Eben at Yale, installed themselves in No. 334 along with four servants—one from Sweden, one from Japan, and two from Hungary. The presence of the domestic workers was typical of the New York wealthy at the time. Many houses had a cook and several maids, who generally lived on the top floor and shared a bathroom. In the upstairs-downstairs arrangement of the time, servants took their meals in the basement. Laundry women came in several times a week for the washing. Tradesmen delivered ice and coal, fruit and vegetables, and other goods. Large receptions were held in the upstairs drawing rooms.

Takamine was also a prominent citizen and a representative of Japanese culture in his adopted country. He was a founding member of the Japan Society. He had the Japanese pavilion—a replica of an eleventh-century Kyoto palace—at the 1904 World's Fair in St. Louis dismantled and reconstructed on land Caroline had bought in the summer resort community of Merriewold, in Sullivan County, New York. He renamed it Sho-Fu-Den, or "Pine Maple Hall," and used it as his summer place, sometimes hosting visiting Japanese royalty. Establishing a retreat at Merriewold was another example of the Hitch family exerting its influence: Caroline's sister, Marie, had a house in the community.

Takamine's public role included helping establish the Nippon Club, and in 1912 he paid for its new home on 93rd street between Columbus and Amsterdam Avenues, now a Seventh-day Adventist Church.

In January 1916, the Takamines held a reception for Eben and his new wife Ethel Johnson at the Cosmopolitan Club. The club was turned into a "Japanese woodland scene" for the gathering of four hundred guests, graced with pine trees, a tiny lake with goldfish and water plants reflecting artificial moonlight, yellow and green lanterns, and a buffet served at a "wayside teahouse" with cherry trees outside.

While the Takamines are obscure in the United States these days, a firsthand account of the family has survived from an unexpected source: an intimate portrait by Agnes de Mille, the great dancer and choreographer who created the steps for Aaron Copland's *Rodeo* and for *Oklahoma!*, among other musicals.

De Mille crossed paths with the Takamines because her parents, William and Anna, were neighbors at Merriewold. De Mille was a prolific memoirist and her 1978 book *Where the Wings Grow* provides a gauzy account of life at the resort, and especially of the Takamines, who inhabited the woodsy refuge as something like a royal family. It's a funny sort of book, a golden-hued bit of nostalgia about a young girl's life in the early years of the last century, quite lyrically written, coupled with a biographical sketch of a highly unusual family of the time. De Mille provides detailed portraits of Jokichi and Caroline and their two sons Jo and Eben. The recollections come some sixty years later and it is hard to know how much the perceptions of a little girl colored the view, but de Mille also drew on the memories of adult relatives and friends from those days.

Caroline, she said, "had the kind of presence that made everyone rise, men of course, but women too, and without knowing who she was, not only in Japan but everywhere she went." An invitation to her house was like a "diplomatic recognition." Tall, not so slender, straight-backed, often dressed in white, Caroline had a queenly—even haughty—presence. She had strong eyebrows, hair swept up into a crown of braids, and a strictness with the servants.

For the young Agnes, Takamine and his upturned waxed mustache inspired awe. At Sho-Fu-Den, he would stand in the vast Japanese garden, "all in white with his scarlet crest of eight arrowheads embroidered on his sleeve, his fresh pink and white skin gleaming beneath his white hair, flicking a scarlet fan, and we thought him the most stylish figure any of us had ever seen," de Mille wrote. He seemed less remote when taking part in all-night poker games and fishing in the stream.

Takamine had an unpleasant side, de Mille reported. He treated his researchers like "upper servants," who were occasionally invited to dinner at 334 Riverside Drive as guest fill-ins—but never their wives. Despite the air of propriety that filled the Takamine home, de Mille said the distinguished scientist impregnated a young Japanese girl and offered Caroline a divorce. She declined.

Like many sons of rich men, Jo and Eben were spoiled, lazy and cynical, in de Mille's telling. She portrayed Jo, the couple's older son, as a callow rake, with precise manners bordering on the unctuous, who roared about Merriewold in a Stutz Bearcat. She seems to have had a crush on him. "Jo was tender and elusive, small and sophisticated, the one the women feared. Eben was taller, bland in a kind of boyish way." De Mille hints at scandals, saying Takamine used his money and standing "to extricate his sons from their more spectacular predicaments," noting that their parents always forgave them in the end.

Although both boys went to Yale, Caroline could do little to help their social standing because of her marriage to a Japanese man. "Not all of her money, her international affiliations, not her intelligence, nor her Southern charm could procure her boys a decent, dignified life. The boys were Japanese and they could never be anything else in this country except by act of Congress. They were Japs. Japs were yellow—and there was the Yellow Peril, as Mr. Hearst kept drumming into us, and there was the Oriental Exclusion Act," de Mille wrote. That would be the William Randolph Hearst who bought a house for his mistress three doors away from the Takamine home.

The Oriental Exclusion Act, also known as the Johnson-Reed Act of 1924, extended limits on immigration imposed in 1917, amid fears about security in the United States fueled by World War I. It also barred all Japanese from immigrating. An influx of Japanese laborers to California in the century's first decade, along with Japan's increased assertiveness—especially in China—after the Russo-Japanese War, had stoked anti-Japanese sentiments. The long-running anti-Japanese campaign by Hearst newspapers provided more poison. Caroline herself lost American citizenship with her marriage to Takamine, de Mille reported. Even in Merriewold, where the Takamines were well-known residents accorded outward respect, residents muttered ugly remarks about the scientist's heritage.

The Takamines sold their townhouse at 334 Riverside Drive in 1921 to a dentist and moved to Passaic, New Jersey. A year later, Takamine, the Japanese entrepreneur and cherry tree lover, mortally ill with liver disease, converted to Roman Catholicism, following in the footsteps of Caroline. Within days Takamine was dead. His body lay in state at the Nippon

Club, draped by Japanese and US flags. The funeral was held at St. Patrick's Cathedral, as befitting such a prominent New Yorker, and Takamine was buried at Woodlawn Cemetery in the Bronx, where a stained glass window on his crypt shows Mt. Fuji. He had divided his wealth equally between Caroline, Jo, and Eben. In his will, Takamine offered his body to science for dissection. Science declined.

Four years after her husband died, Caroline moved to Arizona and married a younger man, and they frittered away her inheritance.

The Takamine sons continued to work in the companies, with the elder Jo, himself a scientist not without talent, serving as president of International Ferment. But a dissolute youth caught up with him. One February night in 1930, after a drunken binge with a nightclub hostess named Helen Fitts, Jo checked in with her to the Hotel Roosevelt. The police found him later that night with a fractured skull on a ledge twelve feet below his fourteenth-floor window. Fitts said she was too drunk even to remember what places they had gone to. Jo died later at the hospital. The police ruled it an accident, but the circumstances were never explained.

With Jo's death, Eben took over the Clifton, New Jersey, lab. He died in 1953—just months after being naturalized under the McCarran-Walter Act. International Ferment was sold to Miles Laboratories, which was acquired by Bayer, which sold it to Solvay of Belgium, which in 1996 sold it to Genencor International. The Clifton lab was razed in the early 1980s and the land developed for housing. Takamine's papers and some objects had been kept at the Miles offices in Elkhart, Indiana, and eventually were moved to a museum in Kanazawa, the town in Japan where Takamine grew up. "The Great People of Kanazawa Memorial Museum" features

Takamine as one of five featured august locals and has in its holdings his death mask, diary, letters, and a set of evening clothes. Daiichi-Sankyo, one of Japan's largest pharmaceutical companies and a successor to Takamine's original Japanese firm, maintains a room at a research center in Shinagawa, Tokyo, that contains Takamine's desk and other personal items. Pfizer now owns Parke, Davis & Co., as Parke-Davis is called today.

CHAPTER 11.

The Getaway:
Bennie Loses a Leg

THE TWO GETAWAY BOATS HEADED WEST, curling around
the thumb of Sea Gate, and then turned east, passing
Brighton Beach in Brooklyn and entering the Rockaway Inlet.
They edged by Breezy Point at the front end of the Rockaway
Peninsula and passed Floyd Bennett Field, heading onward into
Jamaica Bay. So far, everything was going perfectly. The gang
members did not fire a shot. They gathered up the money with
no resistance. All ten were accounted for and they seemed to
be home free, despite an emerging citywide dragnet.

But as the two boats puttered through the gray waters of
the bay, bobbing with their crews of kidnappers, bootleggers,
and thieves and bags filled with cash, a loud thud sounded.
McMahon, on the speedboat, was apparently transferring the
money from the bank bags into burlap sacks when his shotgun
became tangled up in some line. As he sought to extricate it,
he did not notice that a knot had become caught in the gun's
trigger guard. With a tug, the gun went off, firing into his left
leg and blowing off part of his kneecap. John Oley, Stewart,
Manning, and Hughes, scrambling in the well of the speedboat
with a severely wounded comrade, clearly had an emergency to

deal with. They made the best of what they had on hand, using a rope as a tourniquet around McMahon's thigh to stanch the bleeding.

As they approached land, the men in each boat dumped their guns overboard except for one machine gun. Their boats puttered to a stop on the water's edge in Arverne, a community in the Rockaways.

As McMahon lay bleeding in the speedboat, John Oley and Manning loaded the bags of money into a black Dodge truck—a vehicle McMahon used to transport bootleg liquor during Prohibition—that the gang had left nearby the night before. They drove off to an apartment in Queens belonging to a friend of Oley's, taking the remaining machine gun with them. En route, Takamine's adrenaline began pumping through their veins and they went cold with fear: a police siren was heard in the distance. A squad car approached, and Oley and Manning pulled their truck over. But they relaxed when the police car continued on, responding to another call. They turned back onto the road and proceeded, experiencing the first of several close calls that day.

Meanwhile, the other gang members were left to deal with the emergency resulting from Bennie the Bum's accidental gunshot. Originally, the plan was to eliminate the two largest pieces of evidence, the boats, by sinking them, with the gangsters dispersing singly to reduce suspicion. Now they had the bleeding McMahon to deal with. Geary, Wallace, Quinn, and Francis Oley followed the original program and left individually, traveling by bus to a subway stop where a train took them to Manhattan, most probably the Brighton Beach Line (now the Q train). The speedboat was scuttled and Kress was dispatched by taxi to the home of a friend in Far Rockaway to borrow a car.

Hughes and Stewart stayed behind with the wounded McMahon. While Kress was off retrieving the car, they got back into the dory with McMahon to search for liquor, an unpleasant echo of his rumrunning days. They chugged for a mile west and landed close to the Rockaway Park Yacht Club. Stewart climbed out. After a quick walk, he found a saloon and bought a pint of whiskey for their ailing comrade. Then Hughes piloted them back to their original landing spot, where Kress was waiting with the car. Kress and Stewart heaved McMahon inside for the drive back to Manhattan. Hughes scuttled the dory nearby and took public transport home. All of this was happening in broad daylight.

The account of the gang members' movements becomes spotty at this point. After crossing the Queensboro Bridge into Manhattan, McMahon and his companions Kress and Stewart, traversing the width of the borough in the borrowed car, stopped off at Quinn's garage, registered in the name of Marcey Kelly at 635 West 48th Street, where McMahon rested. He must have been in excruciating pain, maybe slightly numbed by liquor. Later, at a rendezvous in Queens, Francis Oley met Stewart and Wallace at Queens Boulevard and 46th Street and gave them $1,000 to pay for a doctor. McMahon was then brought into the care of Madeline Tully, who ran an establishment that was variously described during those years as a gang hideout, a rooming house, and a brothel.

The address: 334 Riverside Drive, the former home of one of Japan's leading scientists and one of the first biotech engineers of the twentieth century, a man whose funeral was celebrated at St. Patrick's Cathedral. Its current main resident was another immigrant, but of an altogether different nature.

Tully was an underworld fixture, a boardinghouse madam who had immigrated with her Slovakian parents in the 1890s.

At the age of twenty, she had the first of two children with her husband, an Irish American salesman twenty years her senior who soon abandoned the family. To support herself, Tully kept lodgers at various West Side addresses. Typically they were recent Russian immigrants, young couples, dressmakers. At 294 Riverside, she let out rooms to a domestic worker, a salesman, and the Italian journalist Amerigo Ruggiero, a former anarchist and correspondent for the Turin daily *La Stampa*. At 334 Riverside, her boarders included an importer of women's hats and dresses named Ella Engel. "In police circles Mrs. Tully has long been regarded as a shrewd, evasive woman, incapable of resisting the high rents she could obtain from shady characters in need of a hideaway," a *Herald-Tribune* reporter wrote.

It was to Madeline that the gang now turned. Holed up in her boardinghouse, they also needed a doctor, someone who could be trusted to be discreet. Their man was Dr. Harry Gilbert.

Gilbert was also a West Sider, but he lived in a tonier section, just off of Central Park on 69th Street. Gilbert had a practice connected to the Broadway theater world in the 1920s, once making the papers as the doctor who treated a Ziegfeld Follies star named Lillian Lorraine when she was hospitalized with a ruptured appendix. But Gilbert was broad-minded in choosing his clientele. Around the time he was summoned to Riverside Drive, he made a similar call to a gambler named Matthew Borzello who had found himself at the Hotel Alba in Midtown with a major inconvenience: his head had been bashed in.

Gilbert had a gift for attracting press attention. The *New York Times* quoted him as an expert about the evils of bootleg liquor, in a not-so-subtle indictment of Prohibition. He had plenty of opportunity to offer observations, the newspaper said, given his patients. With a certain theatricality, he described the death of one young woman: "That girl was killed by her own friends just as surely as if they had pointed guns at her and pulled the trigger, although they chose a less merciful death. They drowned her in liquor. Case after case was sent to her apartment, day after day, for endless parties. She was young, under thirty, but her liver was that of a middle-aged drunkard in days before Prohibition."

The doctor was prone to hyperbole. "A friend gave me a bottle of supposedly good rye not long ago," he told the *Times*. "I splashed a little on the desk in opening the bottle. It took all the finish off."

"I had some liquor analyzed recently, and the laboratory reported that it contained more than the .02 percent of fusel oil [a mixture of alcohols] that the body will tolerate. It was moonshine liquor. The coloring matter was ordinary caramel. It didn't actually contain wood alcohol but it was poisonous none the less. The instances of blindness and sudden death are only a small percentage of the ills caused by this suicidal stuff."

In August 1934, Gilbert engaged in a different sort of medical science: amputation. He was paid the $1,000 procured by Francis Oley to treat Bennie the Bum's leg in a room in an upper floor of the rooming house, with several of McMahon's confederates present. Gilbert's efforts were to no avail and he decided to amputate the limb. But McMahon had lost too much blood, and he died within one day or three—sources vary. He had had some help in easing himself out of this life. McMahon drank enough to be declared drunk by the medical examiner at the time of death.

Gilbert then received another assignment. McMahon's confederates decided to stuff his body into a steamer trunk so it could be disposed of more easily. But McMahon was a bit outsized for the trunk they had procured. So Gilbert was asked to amputate the other leg. The coroner later found, in a negative appraisal of Dr. Gilbert's handiwork, that the crudely hacked off legs were stuffed into empty spaces around the body, which had been folded over to fit in the trunk.

In the middle of this macabre business, the doorbell rang, freezing the men with fear. Three of them crept down the wooden staircase. As two hid next to the inner doorway with guns drawn, the third, Stewart Wallace, opened the door and was confronted by a policeman in the embrace of a woman. The officer, it seems, had accidentally leaned against the doorbell inside the vestibule while kissing his companion. Stewart, wearing a coat over a shirt spattered with McMahon's blood, thought exceedingly quickly. "You ought to be ashamed waking people out of a sound sleep at this hour of the morning," he barked, according to Jack Alexander's *New Yorker* account. "What would the commissioner say if I reported you?" Ignorant of the gruesome proceedings that had taken place just a few floors away, the policeman backed off with his companion.

When the medical work was done, the doctor was paid another $1,500 to cover the costs of McMahon's burial, a false death certificate, and a payoff to an undertaker. The gang took up a collection for the burial.

For whatever reason—inconvenience? greed?—McMahon's burial never took place. Four days later, a caretaker named Tony Tarantino left his home on West 74th Street in Manhattan and walked down the block to a four-story townhouse, occupied by one Louis Stotesbury, a former adjutant general of the New York National Guard. The caretaker planned to clean up a small concrete yard outside the building. But before he could start, Tarantino noticed something unusual: a black tin trunk, studded and trimmed with brass, wrapped in rope and oozing what appeared to be blood. Tarantino called the police. Inside the trunk, they found a nude body face down, its legs detached. The remains were accompanied by a black jacket with gray pinstripes wrapped up in paper and a wad of medical cotton. The only clues were a cleaner's tag and a torn bit of newspaper with a headline that read, "4 Thugs Killed Church Head at Service." A fingerprint check revealed the corpse's identity: Bernard McMahon. His identity was confirmed by his brother John. Nine pellets were embedded in what remained of his left leg. The trunk was found four blocks from the home of Gilbert, the doctor who tried to save McMahon and then amputated his legs.

Police at first had no idea that McMahon had been involved in the Rubel job. In fact, they had ruled out the notion. The trunk seemed to be foreign, lending later credence to the idea that Madeline Tully, the Slovakian-born lodging manager, had provided it. Investigators never figured out where the trunk had been between the time it received McMahon's body and its discovery four days later.

The day after McMahon was disposed of, the gang members gathered at a Queens apartment and divided up the loot, which was contained in packets of common denominations stamped with the total amount on the outside. Manning announced the amounts and Geary tallied them up, arriving at a total figure of $427,950.

Before the money was divided, about $5,000 was subtracted: $2,500 for Gilbert's fees and the rest for Tully and other miscellaneous expenses. The remainder was divided into nine parts of $47,000 each, even though ten men had taken part. That was because the boatmen, Quinn and Hughes, had early on agreed to split a share. They took their $23,500, tossed it into shopping bags, and left. Geary handed out the other shares. John Oley used an empty potato sack as a satchel. Others had brought briefcases or twine and packaging paper. All agreed that McMahon's family should receive his share. There's no evidence that the gang fulfilled the promise.

Two central characters—Manning, an originator of the plan, and Geary, the professional brought in to provide muscle and guidance, were the last two to leave. Carrying valises stuffed with bills, they hailed a taxi and went to the old Pennsylvania Station.

An insurance company immediately reimbursed the businesses that had lost money in the robbery. The crime claimed other casualties: All three guards lost their jobs.

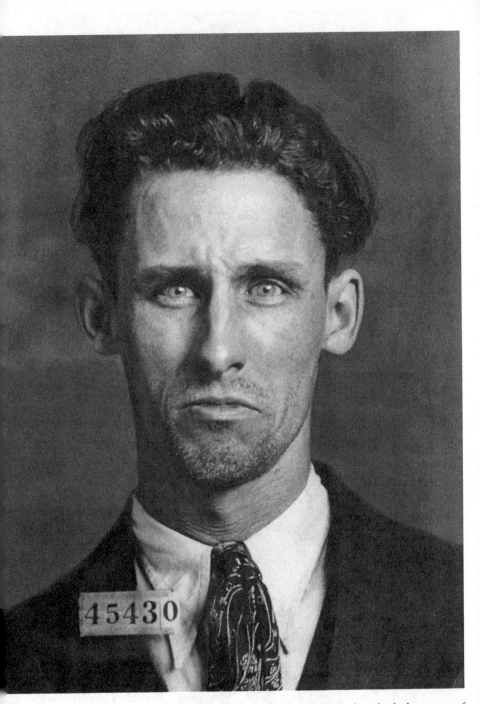

A mug shot of the Rubel gang member Percy Geary, who was wanted in the kidnapping of ohn O'Connell in Albany. The New York Times/Redux.

Joseph Kress handled the wheels for the Rubel gang: he stole the cars used in the heist and drove one of them during the getaway. The New York Times/Redux.

John Oley, right, an Albany hoodlum and Rubel gang member, after being caught following a jailbreak. He is shown handcuffed to a confederate Harold Crowley, with the Syracuse police chief, George Peacock, in the middle. The New York Times/Redux.

Percy Geary was arrested after escaping from the Onondaga County jail. Associated Press.

Bernard McMahon tending bar sometime before the Rubel armored car robbery. He is pictured here possibly in the tavern run by his father. Courtesy of Thomas R. Worsdale.

William O'Dwyer, left, presided as judge in the Rubel heist trial and Burton Turkus served as the defense lawyer for Stewart Wallace. Here, a year later, O'Dwyer is the Brooklyn district attorney and Turkus an assistant DA. The New York Times/Redux.

The Davis family of No. 330 Riverside Drive: Jennie, R. B., and Lulu, below, in photographs that telegraph the family dynamic. It's the baby-faced Lulu who poses with R. B., the old Civil War vet, not his wife. Courtesy of Brenda Steffon.

The Davis family had been living here in 330 Riverside Drive for just two years when this picture was taken.

Dr. Jokichi Takamine, one of the great biochemists of his time, owned No. 334 Riverside Drive. Courtesy of the Great People of Kanazawa Memorial Museum.

Marion Davies, the mistress of No. 331 and William Randolph Hearst, in 1922, the year of her breakout film hit *When Knighthood Was in Flower*. The New York Times/Redux.

The Shakespearean actress Julia Marlowe owned 335 Riverside Drive when she opened the 1905-1906 New York season as Katherine in *The Taming of the Shrew* at the Knickerbocker Theatre. The New York Times/Redux.

CHAPTER 12.

No. 334, Continued: "Four Out of Five Have It"

THIRTEEN YEARS BEFORE THE RUBEL ICE gang used 334 Riverside Drive as a field hospital, it was changing hands from the Takamine family to another self-made success story: Richard Forhan. Forhan was born in 1866 in County Clare, Ireland, to American parents who traveled widely, and he practiced dentistry in Denver, Colorado, for nearly two decades. He developed an astringent to help prevent gum disease for his patients, shared it with colleagues for professional use, and in 1913 brought the formula to New York to try selling it as a consumer product. The astringent eventually became Forhan's Toothpaste, which was promoted with one of the most ubiquitous advertising lines of the 1920s: "Four out of five have it." The "it" was pyorrhea, or gum disease. Forhan sold the company in 1929, but the brand lived on for years, particularly in South America and Europe.

The Forhans were so prominent that Governor Al Smith attended the lavish wedding of one of their three daughters, Rea, in 1927 at the Church of the Ascension, on 107th Street, where David Canavan's funeral had taken place. Mayor Jimmy Walker was also among the wedding guests, along with the police commissioner, George McLaughlin. Rea's husband was William Pedrick, vice president of the Fifth Avenue Association. After a honeymoon in Palm Beach and Nassau, the young couple went to live south of the Seven Beauties at 90 Riverside Drive.

Even years after they left No. 334, the Takamines' stamp remained: the Japanese furnishings and decorations they had lovingly installed. It must have been a treat for the Forhans to live in such an unusually decked-out home. But it turned out not to have been such a blessing.

One night, a year after Rea's wedding, Forhan was away in California on business, leaving his wife home with two maids. It was a cloudy, cold evening in March. A heating duct under the staircase in the basement overheated, causing fireproofing to fall off and setting the carved adjoining woodwork on fire. The flames spread quickly, trapping Mrs. Forhan in her bedroom on the third floor and sending smoke billowing out toward the park. Neighbors clustered on the sidewalk below as she leaned out of her window, on the verge of panic. They shouted for her to wait for the firemen. Meanwhile, the two maids, Delia Morrisey and Marie Holdwig, were stuck on the fifth floor and screamed for help. Mrs. Forhan had called her son-in-law, William Pedrick, as the fire started and he rushed up from his own Riverside home, arriving in pajamas and slippers. He and a fireman ran up the stairs to rescue her from a window ledge. But the blaze was preventing access to the maids, who were leaning, terrified, out of their windows two stories above. So Fireman John McFarland of Hook and Ladder Co. No. 40 climbed up to the roof of either No. 333 or No. 335 next door (reports do not specify) and lowered himself by a rope to their level. Other firefighters extended a section of ladder to them and McFarland reached over and held himself and the two women against it.

All three were lowered to safety. His actions earned McFarland a citation for bravery.

Mrs. Forhan's neighbors, the Faber family in No. 335, took her in for the night. There is no mention of where the maids went to stay. The fire charred much of the Japanese artwork and furnishings that had been left over from the Takamine days.

Forhan spent $200,000 to repair the damage of the fire, but it was not enough to keep him at No. 334, and he put the house on the market. In 1929, the India Society of America, led by Hari G. Govil, a supporter of and correspondent with Gandhi, acquired the option to buy No. 334 for $22,000. The society launched a $300,000 fund-raising campaign to make the purchase, establish an endowment, and turn the townhouse into an India Center, with an auditorium, art gallery, library, and temple brought from India. Nothing came of the plan, a victim of the stock market crash and Depression.

Forhan and his wife divorced in 1932 on grounds of "continuous quarreling." One big quarrel concerned a trust fund he established for his wife and children. Mrs. Forhan sued to gain access to $850,000 in the trust that she said was owed her— money that Forhan invested in a company that controlled No. 334. Forhan finally found a buyer for the townhouse in 1933—the Aeon Realty Co., which flipped it to another real estate concern, the Barlock Realty Co. The proceeds of the sale may have been used to pay Mrs. Forhan's claim.

In 1933, the same year he parted with No. 334, Forhan also sold his waterfront estate in Mamaroneck. Forhan died at his East Side home in Manhattan in 1965, a year shy of his hundredth birthday.

In a curious footnote, No. 334 would have another run-in with the law thirty years after the Rubel gang's gruesome interlude there. Pauline Sargent, twenty-three, who lived at No. 334 in 1968 while a student in the general studies program at Columbia University, had taken part in the protests that swept the campus that spring, including the week-long occupation of five Columbia buildings. Sargent was part of the group that occupied Fayerweather Hall and was arrested when police swarmed through the buildings and broke up the protests. She and fellow student Miriam Ziegellaub were the first two protesters jailed in the Columbia protests when Judge Amos Basel of Criminal Court sentenced them each to fifteen days in prison.

They had pleaded guilty to a trespassing misdemeanor. Judge Basel said the right to dissent was protected by the Constitution, but that those who committed civil disobedience must pay the price. "There were thousands of students who went to Columbia who wanted to go to school, who were not allowed the right of access to their classes and their professors," Basel said. "I don't see any moral justification for this act. The law cannot condone what you did." A Supreme Court judge ordered the two released the next day on $1 bail pending an appeal of the sentences as excessive.

CHAPTER 13.

The Hunt: "A Motion Picture Director's Dream"

WITHIN MINUTES OF THE RUBEL ICE Company robbery, emergency calls quickly reached the police precinct at Bath Avenue and Bay 22nd Street, a four-minute walk away. What ensued was the kind of law enforcement response that today would be reserved for a major terrorist attack.

All available detectives in Brooklyn were summoned. Sirens blasted the air. Assistant Chief Inspector John Sullivan rushed in to Brooklyn from Manhattan. Police cruisers poured through the neighborhood and officers stopped cars with two or more men for questioning. Patrols scouted every highway passing through Brooklyn. Marksmen and squad cars took up positions at the entrances to the three bridges over the East River connecting Brooklyn and Manhattan—the Brooklyn, Manhattan, and Williamsburg spans. Even the Hudson River crossings were watched. When investigators heard from witnesses later in the day that the gang was seen boarding boats, a marine operation was launched. Police boats went on patrol, and two police planes took off from Floyd Bennett Field to survey the waters. Investigators began checking marinas, garages, and yacht basins on Long Island and along the coast. Two Coast Guard cutters were deployed to check anchorages in Long Island Sound and along the Jersey shore. As Jack Alexander wrote in his *New Yorker* piece about the heist, "By nightfall the chase had turned into a motion picture director's dream."

Word came from on high: Mayor Fiorello LaGuardia had personally demanded that the robbers be caught. Sullivan, the assistant chief inspector, predicted that given the amount of money and number of perpetrators involved, solving the crime was inevitable. A former member of the State Crime Commission, Thomas Rice, rather oddly noted that the operation had a flaw: its meticulous planning. "The Brooklyn crime was perfect in preparation, operation and getaway—and that is where the whole scheme may be expected to break down," he said. "It was too elaborate." He proved to be partially right. Adding the wrinkle of the boat escape provided important clues that helped police identify the perpetrators.

Journalists and lawmen displayed an almost breathless admiration for the complexity and success of the plan, a reflection of the way gangsters were mythologized in the 1930s. "I don't know of any instance in my time when the thieves went to so much planning, and everything worked out to perfection," Sullivan told the *Brooklyn Eagle*. The *Eagle*'s Frank Emery, in the lead story on the paper's front page, wrote: "Besides agreeing that the holdup was the most daring and sensational in the city's history, police were also agreed on numerous other points. First, that the perpetrators, from their daring and expert seamanship, were probably former rum runners and hijackers who have been hard-pressed for cash since Prohibition repeal. Second, that the crime was executed to a point of precise perfection, indicating thorough planning of probably several months and direction by a 'master mind' more cunning than a Capone and nervier than a Dillinger. Third, that the getaway seems to have been as thoroughly planned as the execution of the holdup and had probably been completed before the police, at 3:30 p.m., learned that the machine gunners had taken to sea." How right he was on all counts, except perhaps the hyperbolic criminal namedropping.

Dozens of people had witnessed the crime or were in the immediate vicinity, and it was not surprising that confusion reigned about exactly what had happened. Some witnesses said five men jumped out of the cars that were trailing the armored car, others said twelve. Some said that six machine guns were involved. Others thought that three cars were involved. In all, the police took down the names of twenty-two witnesses, including the three guards in the truck. None were able to pick out suspects from mug shots. Either they were shown the wrong mug shots, or their unshaven faces and costumes helped mask the gang members' identities.

At the same time, physical evidence abounded. A key item was the machine gun dropped by Manning and picked up by Lilienthal—but Lilienthal's handling of the weapon obliterated any fingerprints, and the serial number had been filed off. The police went over the pushcart carefully and even found the man who built it—but he could provide no information about its buyer, except that he had paid $10.

The blue Lincoln was found abandoned near Bay 35th Street, close to the Ben Machree Boat Club. Thomas Maitland, a captain who berthed his boat at the club, told police that he saw several men leave the car and jump aboard a mahogany speedboat carrying canvas bags. Other witnesses described events at the shore and gave descriptions of the boats. Loomis Wolfe—who either worked nearby at the Bensonhurst Fuel Distributing Corporation or as the superintendent of lumber yards at Cropsey Avenue, depending on the account—said that in the morning he saw a Lincoln turn off Cropsey onto Bay 35th Street. Several men disembarked from a boat at a nearby pier and got into the car. The Lincoln reappeared shortly after 1:30 p.m., Wolfe said, whereupon two men jumped out, ran to the pier, and hopped aboard a launch. Another witness, described in news reports only as a "Negro" without a name in the casual racism of the day, said he had told the gang members that they were trespassing on private property.

The Lincoln bore stolen license plates and was determined to have been stolen from a Mrs. Anna Friedman of 217 Beverly Road in Brooklyn some three months earlier. The Nash was found three blocks away, at Bay 38th Street. It had pulled up around 12:40 p.m., witnesses said, and several men had gotten out and headed for the water.

In the evening of the day after the robbery, a tugboat captain passed on a tip to the police. Hours after the heist, he said, he saw a man hammering on the hull of a lobster boat, apparently trying to fix it. But after reading the detailed account of the robbery in the newspapers the next morning, the captain read something more suspicious into what he had seen and directed police to where he had observed the boat. Police found the dory, scuttled in Jamaica Bay off Beach 79th Street in Arverne, in the Rockaways.

A check quickly determined that the boat was registered to a John Donahue.

On the fifth day after the heist, another tip led to the discovery of the second boat, the Gar Wood speedboat, off Beach 72nd Street. The registration number had been filed off, and someone had tried to do the same with the motor number. But the job was not thorough enough. Members of the police crime lab were able to raise the numbers. They telegraphed the factory that made the boat. The answer came back: its buyer was, again, a Mr. John Donahue. The boat identifications proved to be an early and critical break in the case.

Donahue's address was given as 635 West 48th Street, the location of the garage owned by Marcey Kelly where the wounded McMahon had been brought. No one there admitted to knowing Donahue. That was because John Donahue did not exist, or at least a boat-owning Hell's Kitchen John Donahue did not exist. Meanwhile, a police detective, starting with the Detroit factory that made the engine, traced the speedboat to a West Side pier, where boaters identified the owner as Thomas Quinn, who occasionally used the pseudonym John Donahue. Quinn was a former rumrunner, the married father of three children, who lived nearby at 501½ West 43rd Street. He had a criminal record that included arrests for illegal possession of a revolver and was a suspect in a saloon shooting.

When the police went to 501½ they discovered that the Quinns had abruptly abandoned the apartment the day after the robbery. The landlord had seized their furniture in place of back rent. Although there was nothing inside the apartment to give the Quinns away, the detectives hit upon an ingenious way to trace their whereabouts. The superintendent of the building knew the names and approximate ages of the couple's children. Children, generally, go to school. So the detectives checked out records of the Board of Education and located the children in upper Manhattan. That information led to the Quinns' new address. Detectives staked out the building in question and followed Quinn's wife when she took the children for walks in Van Cortlandt Park. But she did not lead them to Quinn, who seemed to have vanished. Sources eventually told the detectives that Quinn had relocated to New Jersey, moving from town to town, presumably to avoid capture.

But Quinn could not take the pressure any longer. On November 16, he showed up at police headquarters in the company of a lawyer and offered to clear matters up. He had read about the robbery in the newspapers, including the descriptions of the boats used in the getaway. That information, he said, jogged his memory. Quinn admitted to owning the two boats, and said that Hughes had bought a half-interest in the speedboat. Hughes, he told the investigators, had brought in some unknown men who rented the boats for a fishing expedition. Fearing that he would be implicated, Quinn said, he ran away. Not buying the story, the police arrested Quinn and held him as a material witness. After three months of questioning, Quinn finally admitted knowing that the boats were to be used in a crime, but was steadfast in denying that he took part in the robbery. The police were forced to release him.

Quinn's acquaintances later told detectives that he had been seen in the company of John Oley. Separately, an informant offered to police that Kress, who had stolen the cars for the heist, was interested in a robbery on the waterfront. Police questioned Kress, who refused to crack and denied any involvement in the Rubel case.

Suspicion quickly fell on local criminals. During Prohibition, the waterfront along Bath Beach was controlled by Frankie Uale and Vannie Higgins, who was Brooklyn's top crime boss before dying from an affliction of machine gun fire in 1932. But remnants of the Higgins gang were still hanging on, and given the crew's expertise at running booze-carrying boats across Gravesend Bay and knowledge of secret landing spots along the Long Island and New Jersey coasts, they weren't a bad bet. Police got nowhere on the Brooklyn front, and rumors flew wildly farther afield.

Three days after the robbery, police in Philadelphia arrested two well-dressed men from Brooklyn driving in an Oldsmobile. They were carrying five crisp $100 bills, $75 in smaller denominations, and a revolver. A third man who came to the police station to secure their release was also arrested, and all three were held on suspicion of being part of the Rubel gang. The suspicion turned out to be false, although one of the men was identified as the husband of Clara Phillips, a woman convicted in California as the "hammer murderess," a tabloid sensation of the time.

In Keansburg, New Jersey, a man found a money bag and suspicions arose that it was an important clue—until it was pointed out that the bag had the words FEDERAL RESERVE printed on it, which the stolen bags of money did not.

Coast Guard cutters roamed the coast after a tip came that three men in a boat were seen off Sandy Hook.

New York City investigators continued to scrounge for more evidence, even making fruitless trips around the country. In response to reports that tied one Joseph Burns of Chicago, a man the *Times* quaintly described as a "Midwestern desperado," to the Rubel case, John Ryan, a deputy chief inspector, sent a detective out to Chicago to question Burns. The following May, detectives were dispatched to Providence to question members of a gang arrested for a mail truck robbery in Fall River.

Some of the sharpest and most honored detectives on the New York City police force were assigned to the case. They included Detective Francis Phillips, who at twenty-six had become the youngest officer promoted to first-grade detective. Phillips had arrested Willie Sutton, the bank robber of "Because that's where the money is" fame, not once but twice. He helped capture Francis "Two-Gun" Crowley, a hoodlum responsible for a remarkably large amount of mayhem before being captured at age twenty in a bullet-drenched raid involving more than 100 officers at 90th Street and West End Avenue. He investigated "Legs" Diamond and served as a bodyguard to Mayor Jimmy Walker.

Another star detective leading the case was John Osnato, a gregarious six-foot-three lawman known as Big John who worked out of the Bath Beach police station. Osnato was a major figure in the early decades of the modern New York City police department, a rare Italian to crack the ranks of the heavily Irish American force. A look at his life is worth a digression here.

The young Osnato was a dutiful young man and after graduating from DeWitt Clinton High School around 1908, he followed the wishes of his parents and become an apothecary's apprentice. The police force beckoned, however, and he soon joined the department. In his early years walking a beat in his old Lower East Side neighborhood, Osnato tracked down runaway horses and lost children, but also mixed with local hoodlums with names like Dopey Benny and Lefty Louie.

Still trying to square familial duties with his ambitions for a more exciting life, Osnato again bent to parents' will and left the force to join his father's smelting business as a salesman, a job he held for six years. According to *Lawyer in the House*, a memoir by his son John Osnato Jr., tragedy struck twice in this period: John Jr. was stricken with polio, and Osnato's first wife died of complications related to the birth of their son Dudley.

Osnato returned to the force for good in 1918 and was assigned to the Brooklyn waterfront in what is now Sunset Park, just north of Bay Ridge and several neighborhoods away from Bath Beach. Along with the beat patrolman's tasks—

dealing with domestic violence, keeping an eye out for bur-glaries—he dealt with crimes specific to the waterfront world: bootleggers and foreign sailors robbed by doxies, or prostitutes. Along the way he married again, this time to a fellow member of the police force, Helen Burns.

In 1919, Osnato was promoted to plainclothes detective. As Geary, Oley, McMahon, and other members of the gang were embarking on criminal careers courtesy of Prohibition, Osnato was arresting bootleggers, busting saloons, and investi-gating gang-related murders. Within several years he became a detective second grade. Throughout, Osnato honed his ability to cultivate informants, an invaluable skill when it came to tracking down the Rubel robbers. The basic principle involved acquiring credit: overlooking minor crimes or releasing the lesser members of a criminal group with the promise that they would help him in the future. It was an investment strategy.

Osnato developed a virtuoso ability to create and cultivate stool pigeons, through a mix of charm and threat. He paid infor-mants. He played the good cop, "rescuing" a suspect from rough handling by his colleagues. With Italian suspects, he spoke in their language. He never met informants in public places or in the police station, and if one was arrested, Osnato would smack him around to avoid betraying his status in front of others.

In 1925, Osnato crossed paths with Al Capone. On Christmas morning of that year, the detective and his col-leagues received a tip about a shooting at the Adonis Social Club, a speakeasy near the Gowanus Canal in Red Hook.

The club had been founded in 1917 with the aim of bringing together Italian and Irish veterans of the Great War, although Italians dominated. This laudable goal was set against the backdrop of vicious strife between Italian and Irish mobsters for control of the lucrative Brooklyn waterfront. The Italian gang, precursors of the modern Mafia, was called the Black Hand, and was led by the noted gangster Frankie Yale (Ioele). Their Irish opponents were dubbed the White Hand, commanded by William "Wild Bill" Lovett, a World War I machine gunner who had received a Distinguished Service Cross. The Italian–Irish strife led to more than 100 murders between 1915 and 1925, few of them solved.

Lovett was murdered in 1923—shot and cleavered in the head, his assailant known only by the Sicilian moniker Due Cuteddu, or Two Knives. Lovett's brother-in-law, Richard Lonergan, took over. Lonergan, known as Peg Leg because of a childhood streetcar accident that severed a limb, was a vicious killer and a hater of Italians whose own mother fatally shot his father in a fight.

Before decamping to Chicago, Capone frequented the Adonis and was said to use its basement as a firing range. Around Christmas of 1925, he had returned to New York with his wife to have doctors operate on his young son for a mastoid bone infection. Capone was at the club that Christmas Eve, where celebrating was underway. Lonergan came in with five confederates. Drunk and abusive, they began shouting rude epithets. When three Irish girls arrived with Italian dates, Lonergan reportedly yelled, "Come back with white men, fer Chrissake!" Gunfire erupted and Lonergan was killed instantly, his loaded .38 pistol undrawn and a toothpick still in his mouth as he lay dead. Two of his men were killed, one found near the piano and the other in the gutter just outside. Ten people, including Capone, were eventually arrested, although the charges were dismissed. But suspicion lingered that Capone had been summoned to finish off Lonergan once and for all. Osnato was there to investigate, and was given credit for arresting Capone.

Yale's turn came two and a half years later when he was found shot to death in his car in Bay Ridge. No one ever assumed his mantle, though Osnato's informants fed him a steady supply of tips about the pretenders to the throne.

Osnato took part in a string of other highly publicized cases in the years leading up to the Rubel robbery. In 1927, he was assigned to investigate the holdup of a poker game where the victims were ordered to take off their pants to stop them from interfering with the getaway of the stickup men. In another poker game holdup, Osnato and his partners arrested a suspect in Harlem, induced him to talk, and gathered up six other accomplices. In 1928 he traveled to Wallingford, Connecticut, to arrest a plasterer who fatally shot a Brooklyn woman in her home while she prayed at a private altar. The plasterer blamed the devil.

In 1930, Osnato helped arrest a group of kidnappers in a case that would have parallels to the O'Connell affair up in Albany. This time, the victim was the son of Pasquale Gandolfo, a wealthy baker. The son, twenty-two-year-old Louis Gandolfo, was grabbed, brought to a safe house, and forced to write ransom notes to his father. Pasquale's brother-in-law served as the go-between, but was in fact in league with the kidnappers. Pasquale paid $7,000 of a $10,000 ransom demand, which was enough to free his son. He reported the kidnapping only after the gang came back a few months later and demanded the $3,000 balance.

A year later, Osnato handled an entirely different sort of case. For months, bombs had been mysteriously exploding at theaters around the Northeast. An explosion at a Brooklyn apartment brought the detective to the scene, where two unemployed stagehands had been injured. They and several others were arrested in a campaign of violence by union members against the theaters.

Later, when one of his fellow rookie cops—William O'Dwyer—was Brooklyn district attorney, Osnato would serve as a leading investigator in the case brought by O'Dwyer's office to break up Murder, Inc., also known as the Combination—a Brooklyn-based band of killers that industrialized murder for hire on behalf of Jewish and Italian mobsters. It was Osnato who set the dominos of confession falling. The low-level gang member Dukey Maffetore had been arrested in connection with the killing of a fellow gangster. Repeatedly visiting Maffetore in his cell, Osnato spoke to him in Italian and gave him cigarettes. He probed for a weak spot, pointing out that higher-ups in the mob were living well, in contrast to Dukey's street corner existence. Working his magic, he induced Maffetore to cooperate. Maffetore named a culprit in the killing. Word of the cooperation reached Abe "Kid Twist" Reles, the leader of the Brownsville faction of Murder, Inc. So Reles asked to see O'Dwyer and eventually unburdened himself of a vast amount of information about wrongdoing— including some sixty-three murders.

Osnato and O'Dwyer ended up becoming close friends, living just a few blocks from each other in Brooklyn, according to the younger Osnato. Osnato Sr. had a canny sense of how the system worked, and how favor-trading kept careers moving, advising his son to take a low-paying job as a criminal defense attorney because he knew that his connections to O'Dwyer would bring in clients. Big John had sent his son to seek O'Dwyer's advice about going to law school. The young Osnato went back to O'Dwyer after graduating from Columbia Law, and O'Dwyer put in a word with an assistant district attorney, Burton Turkus, to help find him a job. As it turned out, both Turkus and O'Dwyer would figure prominently in the Rubel case.

One question loomed over the Rubel heist investigation: Was it an inside job? Probably not, declared William Dempsey, the United States Trucking executive, who insisted that the guards in the armored car were above reproach. The Federal Reserve had also made it difficult for guards to collaborate with thieves primarily because, according to the Fed's guidelines, armored car guards were not told their specific route until the morning of the work day, when the driver was given a sealed envelope with his orders as the car's engine revved up.

Dempsey may have publicly attested to the honesty of the guards, but either he did not believe his own words or the company lost confidence in the armored car crew. Three months after the robbery, the company fired Lilienthal without explanation. A father of seven, Lilienthal went public with a lament, telling the *Eagle* two years later that he was unable to find a job as an armed guard. Not unexpectedly, the man who stared at machine gun barrels and then went in pursuit, firing back at the thieves, turned on his former employer and said he had refused to help in the investigation, declining—a year after the heist—to travel to Pompton Lakes, New Jersey, to view possible suspects.

"After the rotten deal they gave me, I see no reason why I should jeopardize the lives of my seven children and my wife to help those who have had no consideration for me," he told the newspaper. "I am afraid that if I was to identify anyone my kids might get hurt, or I might be shot in the back or hit over the head coming home some night." He added ominously, wielding the only weapon available to someone in his position, "I am fast forgetting that there ever was a robbery."

Over the next few years, rumors continued to surface about the case, including that John Dillinger was responsible, even though he was killed a month before the robbery. The police had so far been unable to catch up with the gang members, but violence had its own way of finding them. Lilienthal's fears may not have been unreasonable.

CHAPTER 14.

No. 335: "Freedom Was Mine"

IT IS EASY TO PASS BY 335 Riverside Drive without noticing its humble elegance and charming slimness. Closer inspection reveals the subtle confidence with which it registers. First, No. 335 is red brick, unlike the grays and beiges of its neighbors. And in contrast to the block's Beaux-Arts flavor, it is in the Colonial Revival style, unusual in the neighborhood. Fluted columns supporting a balcony stand in front of a classical porch. "The neo-Palladian window on the parlor floor has Ionic columns and pilasters and a scallop-shell arch surmounting its cornice," the Landmarks Preservation Commission noted approvingly many years later. "Two heavy garlands are set on the wall just above the third-floor windows. The sixth floor still has its original lead-covered dormers although the cornice below them has been removed."

Despite its self-effacing nature, 335 Riverside is connected to some of the block's most fascinating history. In 1903, a single woman took ownership. She was Julia Marlowe, who had divorced her husband just three years earlier and was now hurtling toward the celebrity of being America's most famous

Shakespearean actress. But the house remained lonely because Marlowe was constantly on the road.

She had been born Sarah Frances Frost in 1866, in Caldbeck, a village in the English Lake District, and ended up in the United States due to a family mishap. The newspaperman Charles Edward Russell, in a fawning 1926 biography, *Julia Marlowe: Her Life and Art*, told the story. Her father, a storekeeper named John Frost, perhaps drunk and flush with a winning day at the races, engaged in an impromptu horse-and-buggy race with another driver and cracked his whip in triumph as he passed by his opponent. "You have knocked out my eye!" the man screamed. Russell described what happened next: "Panic terror seized upon John Frost. Visions of jail, the county assizes, life imprisonment or even the gallows possessed him." Hence the need for immediate escape, which as it turned out proved unnecessary. The other driver was faking his injury.

However invalid the reason, the fearful Frost adopted his mother's maiden name of Brough, made his way to Liverpool, and boarded a ship bound for America. His wife Sarah followed with their four children, including the six-year-old Sarah Frances, in 1872. Adopting the new family surname, Sarah Frances became Fanny Brough. The family began their American life in Olathe, Kansas, near Kansas City, where John Brough opened a store. After several moves along the frontier, the Broughs eventually settled in Cincinnati.

One aspect of Midwestern cultural life at the time were operettas performed by children, productions that toured from town to town. According to Russell, the eleven-year-old Fanny answered a newspaper ad for a child-cast production of Gilbert and Sullivan's *H.M.S. Pinafore*. She was accepted and began a long tour, making her debut as a "Pinafore" sailor in Ironton,

Ohio. A theatrical manager took her in hand, and by eighteen, Fanny Brough had played as many roles. Acting and singing lessons, a carefully conceived stage name, big Shakespearean roles: Sarah Frost knew exactly what she wanted—stardom under a proscenium.

With the help of her mentor and teacher, the actress Ada Dow, Sarah, who was now calling herself Julia Marlowe, arranged for a one-time only appearance at the Bijou Theater in 1887 to introduce herself to the New York theater world. In this production, she played Parthenia, the heroine of *Ingomar, the Barbarian*, a potboiler romance set in ancient Greece. Parthenia, the daughter of the captured Greek Myron, instructs the barbarian chieftain Ingomar in the art of sentimental love. The part included the memorably mawkish couplet, "Two souls with but a single thought / Two hearts that beat as one," often incorrectly attributed to the poet John Keats. The theater critic for *The New York Times*, Edward A. Dithmar, was captivated and wrote: "Julia Marlowe: remember her name, for you will hear of her again."

Next came *Twelfth Night* and *Romeo and Juliet*. Marlowe toured, returned to New York, and then scored a major commercial success as Mary Tudor, the sister of Henry VIII, in the drama *When Knighthood Was in Flower*, which she also directed. The play, which was adapted from a novel that, as noted, would also become the inspiration for the hit silent movie featuring Marion Davies, the future occupant of 331 Riverside Drive, ran for six months in 1901, and Marlowe reprised it the following season. "I had about as 'starry' a part as anyone could aspire to," she was given to say in *Julia Marlowe's Story*, a first-person hagiography by her future husband and longtime acting partner, Edward Hugh Sothern. "Indeed Mary Tudor was on the stage from the rise of the curtain in each of the four acts till its fall. Every mood of all the characters I had ever played seemed packed into its compass. The public wanted 'pep,' and here it was by the bucket and cartload."

"From the moment Mary Tudor entered," Julia continued in this starry-eyed account, "I felt assured and in high feather. I went from act to act with spirits unbounded and unflagging. The play was bringing within my grasp all I had longed for through so many hard-working years. Freedom, independence, the right to choose without restraint. That greatest of all blessings, the direction of my own will, and the right to seek happiness in my own way. How I had waited, longed for this moment! As the curtain rose and fell the audience applauded and finally broke out into cheers. My whole body throbbed with the exertion and the sense of victory."

That first season alone, she continued, "made me a fortune sufficient to render me independent for the rest of my life," adding, "The second season I more than doubled it. Freedom was mine." Russell, the newspaperman who describes himself in his book as Marlowe's main business advisor, estimated that after just a few weeks of the run her earnings amounted to $50,000.

The fortune paid for a mansion in Highmount, New York, a town in the Catskills where she spent the summer of 1901. "I began to feel that I had taken root in the world," Marlowe says in her book. Russell, for his part, depicts her as a woman yearning for a home, "a place into which she could go and shut the door and shut out with it the world of struggle and noise." As it turned out, that home was beckoning on Riverside Drive. In the fall of 1903, Marlowe paid $68,000, mostly in cash, for 337 Riverside Drive and its 8,500 square feet, according to the *Real Estate Record*, or the equivalent of $1.8 million nowadays (in today's New York real estate market, it would probably go for many times that).

Note the address: 337 Riverside Drive, according to the *Real Estate Record.* Not 335. In fact, every written reference to Marlowe's house starting the year she bought it through many decades afterward listed it as No. 337 — including the hardcover edition of this book. But a sharp-eyed reader and neighborhood historian, Gil Tauber, suggested that the *building number* did not match the *lot number* of the property, according to New York City's arcane system of identifying building locations. And he was right. What Marlowe had bought was 335 Riverside Drive, not No. 337. A deeper dive into dusty city records uncovered the source of the error: the scribes of the original document recording the property transfer to the actress and her mortgage document mistakenly noted its house number as 337.

Despite her professed yearning for a home, Marlowe may never have actually settled in her Riverside Drive house permanently. That was the conclusion of Russell, who wrote a half-dozen years later that she "at last reluctantly sold it." This is not surprising; she spent much of her time on the road, performing in regional theaters and in London. The *New York Sun* reported on May 16, 1906, that Marlowe was at home "under the care of her physician, Dr. J. E. Stillwell," after being forced to cancel performances of *Romeo and Juliet* in Ottawa because of illness. The *New York Tribune* elaborated, writing, "It was given out that she was suffering from a nervous breakdown." The *Tribune* also reported rumors that Marlowe and Sothern had argued, or that they did not like the arrangements for a forthcoming engagement at the Academy of Music in Brooklyn and wanted to be released from the commitment.

Representatives of the actress engaged in what today would be called spin control, strenuously denying the rumors.

"Freedom, independence, the right to choose without restraint," Marlowe had written. What a contrast to another actress, Marion Davies, whose career received a boost from the same narrative source, *When Knighthood Was in Flower*, a movie by that title just a few years later. Freedom? Independence? The right to pursue happiness in her own way? None of these ever came within Davies's grasp, no matter how successful she became in the eyes of the public. Both women found success and financial reward, but Marlowe was truly independent while Davies remained trapped in a gilded cage of her own, the one constructed by William Randolph Hearst.

A third female contemporary on the block, Lucretia Davis, took another path to self-sufficiency: marriage. Marlowe did not need the protection of a man because of her talent. Davies seized on one regardless of talent, and lived forever with the taint of shame of being a kept woman. Lucretia Davis found independence another way, through a respectable marriage to a solid citizen who took on the stewardship of her birthright, a baking soda company. Remarkably, Lucretia and Julia shared the same photo spread in the January 13, 1907, edition of *The New York Times*. On the left page, Marlowe's portrait appears under the headline "Popular with New York Theatregoers." On the right, we see Lucretia, grouped with "Some Well Known Society Folk."

In 1904, Marlowe and Sothern began their reign as the great Shakespearean couple of the era. They married in 1911 (Marlowe's first marriage, to the actor Robert Taber, had lasted from 1894 to 1900). Her greatest roles included Viola in *Twelfth Night* and Julia in *The Hunchback* by James Sheridan Knowles. Marlowe officially retired from the stage in 1916 but made occasional appearances until 1924. The final chapters of her life were subdued. After Sothern died in 1933, Marlowe went into seclusion, emerging only in 1944 to open an exhibition of her costumes and memorabilia at the Museum of the City of New York. She died in her apartment at the Plaza Hotel in New York on November 12, 1950.

Marlowe was famed for her rich, musical voice, which she exercised while practicing her parts during long walks through Central Park. With her square, heavily cleft chin, strong jaw, and expressive eyebrows, Marlowe was not considered conventionally beautiful, but observers admired the expressiveness of her face. The humorist and theater critic Robert Benchley wrote, "Julia Marlowe has the unique distinction of being the only living actress who has kept me awake throughout an entire performance of Shakespeare." Arthur Symons, a British critic, said she was "not only lovely as Juliet, she was Juliet." A series of Victrola recordings from the early 1920s of Shakespeare scenes by Sothern and Marlowe reveal a warbling, crooning, R-rolling style of recitation that sounds quaint to modern ears but was clearly considered the peak of artistry in their day.

Amid the attention given to New York's Italian, Irish, and Jewish immigrants, it is sometimes overlooked that for decades, Germans constituted one of the largest groups of new arrivals to the United States, including nearly 1 million in the 1850s and nearly 1.5 million in the 1880s, the two peak decades. The city's German-born population reached its height in 1900, at 324,000, nearly one-tenth of the citizenry. A visible symbol of that presence is a statue a Spaldeen's throw away from the Riverside Drive townhouses. It depicts Brigadier General Franz Sigel, a mediocre Union general in the Civil War whose chief talent was helping attract large numbers of German

immigrants to the Union cause. Sigel had military training at
Karlsruhe, took the revolutionary side in 1848, and fled after
the uprising was crushed, eventually arriving in the United
States. Opposed to slavery, he was recruited by the Union in a
campaign to attract abolitionist immigrants to the war effort.
After the Civil War, Sigel edited widely read German newspapers and died on August 21, 1902, exactly thirty-two years
to the day before the Rubel robbery. The statue, dedicated in
1907, depicts Sigel sitting ramrod straight on his horse and
staring across Riverside Drive right at New Jersey. He would
have been a proud neighbor for the several prominent German-
American figures, including William Ahnelt, who took their
place among the occupants of the Seven Beauties.

Another of those German neighbors, the patriarch of a
large, fascinating, tragedy-marked family, traced his roots back
to the middle of the eighteenth century.

In 1761, a thirty-year-old carpenter in the Bavarian town
of Stein, near Nuremberg, set up a small pencil-making concern. The carpenter, Kaspar Faber, did well, figuring out ways
to escape the strict commercial controls of the Nuremberg
authorities. On his death in 1784, his son Anton Wilhelm
Faber took over the business and expanded it. Anton followed
the example of his father, passing on the factory to his son
Georg Leonhard Faber in 1810.

Georg still made pencils his grandfather's way—smelting
lead and encasing it in sticks of wood—while manufacturers
in France improved on the leads and British producers used
a higher quality graphite. So Georg dispatched one of his
sons, Lothar Faber, to London and Paris, where he learned
the French method of blending pulverized graphite and clay,
which made the lead more durable and produced a better line
on paper.

When his father died in 1839, Lothar came home to run the company started by his great-grandfather and instituted the new process. He brought other modernization: new factory buildings, a high-quality graphite supply from a Siberian mine, and a savings bank, pension plan, and discount food store for workers, along with homes and health insurance for them. He did not depart from all tradition, especially in the assignment of gender roles. Male employees handled heavy manual work, while women polished, stamped, and packaged the pencils. That stamp was "A.W. Faber," named for Lothar's grandfather. (Georg also established a tradition of Fabers naming their sons Lothar and Eberhard, presenting a singular challenge to anyone attempting to write about the family. So be prepared.)

Georg had sent Lothar's younger brother Eberhard to the United States to procure red cedar from Florida for the plant in Stein. Eberhard bought a tract of forest on Cedar Key, on Florida's Gulf Coast, and set up a sawmill there. Eberhard then moved to New York and by 1850 was operating a pencil and stationery store at 133 William Street, near Wall Street. Eleven years later, the company was granted a United States trademark for its lead pencils and that year opened America's first pencil factory, near the East River at 42nd Street.

By then, economics dictated a better system for making pencils: sending lead from Stein to be combined with the cedar at a New York factory. When fire destroyed the factory in May 1872, Eberhard Faber established a bigger plant in Greenpoint, Brooklyn, although the company's headquarters remained in lower Manhattan. In 1858, the company began making rubber bands and rubber erasers at a plant in Newark, New Jersey.

Eberhard died on March 2, 1879, at which point his namesake son Eberhard and his younger son Lothar Washington Faber took over the company's United States operations.

Eberhard became president of the firm just a year after graduating from Columbia University, where he studied mining and civil engineering. Strife between the German parent company and its American corporate offspring grew, however, and in 1898, the US branch broke away and was incorporated as the E. Faber Pencil Company. That year, Lothar W. Faber succeeded his brother as president. The German parent company, A.W. Faber, sued over the name, and six years later, the US branch became the Eberhard Faber Pencil Company.

During Lothar W. Faber's tenure, the company more than doubled the floor space at its Brooklyn factory, introducing innovative products like fountain pens, mechanical pencils, and lead refills. The Greenpoint factory eventually encompassed two square blocks, remaining there until 1956, when it moved its offices and operations to Wilkes-Barre, Pennsylvania.

Lothar Washington Faber—the nephew of the Lothar Faber who had built the pencil firm in Germany into a major company and who himself was the great-great-grandson of the company's founder, Kaspar Faber—was not yet forty when he assumed control of the family firm. Armed with a patriotic middle name, he yoked the Faber family to another important German-speaking clan by marrying Anna Prieth. Anna's father, Benedict Prieth, who was born in the Austrian Tyrol and spent time in jail for his revolutionary political sympathies, eventually left the country and settled in Newark in 1857. He founded the New Jersey *Freie Zeitung*, a major newspaper for New Jersey's German immigrants, and edited it until his death in 1879. His wife Theodora, Anna's mother, then took over the paper. With her demise, it passed into the hands of two of her sons—both of whom were accused of treason, amid a wave of anti-German sentiment, because of the paper's opposition to American entry into World War I. This was a branch of the family that made sentences, rather than the implements to write them. There would be other wordsmiths, two of whom decades later would present warm and vivid portraits of Lothar Faber.

Lothar and Anna bought 335 Riverside from Julia Marlowe at the beginning of 1907. They lived there with two of their children: Margaret and Lothar Eberhard (what else?), who later dropped the Lothar, thus making things even more confusing. The household also included three servants, a lodger at times, children and grandchildren for extended periods, and most likely a healthy supply of pencils. It is not hard to imagine the interior of No. 335 adorned with decorations featuring a pencil motif, as was the home of a cousin in the German branch living in Stein.

In 1913, the Fabers at No. 335 announced the engagement of Margaret to Brock Putnam, a scion of the G. P. Putnam's Sons publishing company. That June, the couple were united in a small wedding in the house, attended by just members of the two families and "a few intimate friends," *The Times* reported. At one point the young couple moved to California, where Putnam worked in the sugar beet business near Sacramento, and lived in various military bases around the country after Brock joined the army, rising eventually to the rank of colonel. (Brock later boasted of holding the world record for golf endurance: 252 holes in one day, at the Plainfield Country Club in New Jersey. He stopped playing only once to change his clothes and eat a meal.)

The Putnams and their son, Peter, then eight, moved into the house in 1928 several months after the death of Anna. It is thanks to Peter, who grew up to become a memoirist with an extraordinary story of his own, that we have one of several incisive portraits of Lothar, the patriarch, and of life in the sprawling Faber family. The sketch came in Peter's 1957 memoir "Cast Off the Darkness."

Lothar, whom Putnam called Goppy, served as a powerful figure in the family. "He was not a tall man, but he was deep in the chest and his voice seemed to derive its timbre from the fullness of his frame," Putnam wrote, "just as his conversation gathered inner resonance from the fullness of his life." His thick mustache bristling, Faber would expound on the solar system, evolution, the age of sailing ships and the time he met the great heavyweight John L. Sullivan. He performed calisthenics every morning of his life.

Faber displayed an impish sense of humor—"pure and elemental," Putnam called it—behind a severe bearing, chastising young Peter with mock seriousness for leaving a piece of clothing on the floor and then, in the middle of an admonishing stare, crossed one of his blue eyes toward his nose to signal that he was only teasing. Grandfather and grandson shared a room at the time, and one of Faber's favorite gags was to stand in front of the mirror, his beard shaved and hair brushed, adjust his coat and vest over a starched shirt and collar, and ask the lad, "Well, roommate, are you ready to go down?" The only thing missing was Faber's pants.

The two were close. Faber often took his grandson with him on his travels, including five journeys to Europe by the time Peter was fourteen. Every week, Lothar would weigh himself and then Peter on the standing bathroom scale and mark the numbers down on a shirt cardboard. The ritual continued even when Peter had grown up and came back for visits.

Putnam takes us inside 335 Riverside with a lyrical description of the front bedroom he shared with Goppy. A shade and gold curtains shielded one of the two windows. "The view from the other was blocked by a standing screen, but the sun's rays refracting on the gleaming surfaces of the traffic below reflected moving shadows on a portion of the ceiling," he wrote. "Actually, these were not shadows at all, but reflections of color. I could tell when a large green blur moved across the trapezoid of white above the window that a Fifth Avenue bus was passing, and this was always somehow gratifying." Faber, wearing a white nightshirt and green terrycloth slippers, would then open the curtains and shade and move the screen. "We stood for a moment, each at his window, to gaze at the beauty of the morning," Putnam continued. "The Hudson spread its broad surface for a mile to the sheer rock cliff of the palisades, rising through an atmosphere so miraculously clear that the very branches of the trees that crowned them seemed to wink at us."

What is most remarkable about these evocative passages, and many other vivid descriptions in his memoir, is that Putnam was blind when he wrote them.

This is what had happened. At the end of his junior year at Princeton, weighted down by depression, a feeling of aimlessness and a sense of inadequacy partly fueled by the burden of family expectations and the conviction that he could never escape the pencil company, Putnam shot himself in the head with a .22-caliber rifle. Although he recovered from the wound, he did enough damage to his optic nerve to lose his sight. "Cast Off the Darkness" is an account of Putnam's recovery and his newfound sense of purpose. He returns to Princeton, graduates, earns a doctorate in history, marries and has three children and becomes a writer and teacher.

In one of the most touching passages in the book, Putnam describes the first visit from his grandfather since the "accident," on the occasion of his twenty-first birthday. Lothar Faber takes his gold pocket watch, which he himself received on his twenty-first birthday six decades before, and plays a hoary game with a young relative—blow on it and magically, it springs open (with the secret press of a button). He puts the watch in Peter's hand to demonstrate the trick, and then casually asks him to feel the face. The crystal is missing, and Peter asks if it is broken. "Can you tell what time it is?" Lothar responds. Peter gently touches the hands and correctly answers: ten minutes to five o'clock. "That's yours," his grandfather says. "Keep it. It's your birthday present."

"I tried to think of all the physical articles that I associated with my grandfather," Putnam wrote, "and none of them seemed nearly so fitting a symbol of his character as this watch—simple, precious, dignified, the plaything of his grandchildren and the timepiece by which he had regulated the movements of his orderly and constructive life."

Faber's rectitude, as well as his kindness, emerges from another family member's written recollection of life at No. 335.

"In a way, he was a kind of one-man Good Housekeeping Institute or Consumers' Research, before whom things, people, and moral attitudes passed in review, to be ticketed or not with the seal of approval," Benedict Thielen wrote. Faber looked with favor on rye but not scotch, French cuisine but not French morals, "most things Germans" but not German-Americans, European standards in food but not European decadence, America's democratic virtues but not its puritanism and Prohibition.

Thielen, who was Brock Putnam's first cousin, was a novelist and magazine writer who came from the Prieth branch of the family. His mother was Anna's sister, and Lothar was his uncle. Just about the time Peter Putnam was finishing his memoirs, Thielen, who grew up in Newark, contributed his own recollections of childhood visits to the house on Riverside Drive with an article published in *The New Yorker* in 1956.

As seen through a child's eyes, it was a magnificent house, striking from the moment Thielen passed through the "iron-scrolled front door into the marble entrance hall." He continued: "The gold and maroon velvet of Florentine chairs glowed darkly against brocaded walls. Marble nudes lurked in corners. A bust of Lincoln smiled its sad smile from the top of a piano.

"On a pedestal, a hand-carved wooden horseman was eternally poised to spear a wild boar. There were tapestries and embroideries, fans of Spanish lace and locked rococo cabinet filled with minute, mysterious objects of—I was sure—incalculable value. Enormous paintings made windows in the walls through which I saw breathtaking vistas of the Alps and the Bay of Naples. In the dining room, the pictures were horns of plenty that spilled out fruit and fish and flowers."

In a sense, the house, and Riverside Drive itself, represented the most vivid parts of Thielen's childhood. From its windows, he watched parades by the 7th Regiment, home of New York's social elite and headquartered at its ornate and elegant armory on Park Avenue; a flotilla of the Atlantic Fleet; and sightseeing visits by tourists who came to gawk at the former home of Julia Marlowe.

Inside, the house was often filled with painters and musicians and various eccentrics, many of them Austrian relatives or friends who were "often titled, always charming, usually short of cash." Monocles glittered, wooden swords clacked on the roof during dueling practice, compatriots came for jobs or free lodging. One cousin often left meals in a sulk, another had a dueling scar, another arrived in a sputtering Fiat roadster that he would race through the streets. A loyal butler named Franz, often drunk, would be continually fired and rehired. He was from Croatia; the cook, Matilda, was German and the maid Dolfie was Austrian. (Her two "obese and lethargic" cocker spaniels were named Bismarck and Siegfried.) The whole arrangement resembled a mini-Austro-Hungarian Empire. "I'm sure that Sothern and Marlowe, remembering the resounding speeches they once rehearsed within those walls, would have listened to us with interest," Thielen wrote. And Uncle Lothar tolerated this swirl of theatrics with good humor.

In 1943, the cosmopolitan, polyglot joy abruptly drained from 335 Riverside Drive. After a brief illness, Lothar W. Faber died in the townhouse in which he had lived for nearly four decades. Putnam recalls the deathwatch outside his uncle's bedroom, the one they had shared for a time, along with his effort to fight back tears at the funeral and Faber's "unfailing independence and courtesy and humor."

Lothar's son, known as Ebe, was now the heir apparent at the pencil factory. He was a 1915 Princeton graduate and before that a student at the venerable Collegiate School on the West Side of Manhattan (which was my own alma mater and another eerie connection between me and those buildings). After many years of childlessness, his wife, Julia, had finally given birth to the future inheritor of the Faber pencil crown, Eberhard IV, given the nickname Timmie—taking the pressure off of Peter as the presumptive heir. But a tragedy intervened, complicating the centuries-old tradition of Faber sons taking over for their fathers, and dealing Peter another blow.

The extended Faber family was at their summer home on the Jersey shore, in Mantoloking, one late August day in 1945. Timmie, eight, was standing waist-deep in the mild surf when a sudden current dragged him out to sea. His father, Ebe, jumped in after him, and Brock, Peter's father, followed. So did Duncan Taylor, the boy's maternal uncle. Taylor emerged carrying Timmie ashore, but the two men, Brock Putnam and Ebe Faber, drowned. "What was there purer, what lovelier, what of better report than the spontaneous gallantry of these two men leaping forward under a blue and gold sky toward death in the infinite sea?" Putnam wrote.

Faber's widow, Julia Taylor, was named a vice president of the pencil concern and member of the management committee in 1953 and helped run the company until her son Timmie, Eberhard IV, was old enough to take on responsibility a few years before the move to Pennsylvania. The occasional tug of war between the German and American branches of this kingdom of pencils was resolved in 1987, when the German company's successor, A.W. Faber-Castell, bought the Eberhard Faber Pencil Company in the United States, creating a unified German concern for the first time in nearly a century.

CHAPTER 15.

The Gang Disintegrates: "I Lived High, Wide, and Handsome"

FOR ALL THE INTRICATE PLANNING OF the Rubel robbery, for all the inability of the police to make arrests, the luck of the gang ran out remarkably quickly. Within four years of the heist, all but two of the gang were dead or in jail. McMahon, he of the self-inflicted wound, was of course the first to go. Another confederate was a suicide. Another was mysteriously shot dead. Two were ensconced in the notorious prison on Alcatraz Island. And two more robbed a bank and were quickly caught.

Ever since the robbery, Manning had been keeping a low profile, befitting his quiet demeanor. On the evening of July 9, 1936, a sultry night when people were outside on roofs, stoops, and fire escapes to evade the heat, Manning was walking along 108th Street, near Second Avenue in East Harlem. Someone stepped out of a tenement doorway and fired five shots at him. The bullets left two holes in Manning's back, a third in his chest and a fourth in his left arm. The wounds were fatal.

One voice that could tell police about what had happened that dramatic August day in Bath Beach was silenced, but a motive for Manning's killing never emerged. Some speculated gang rivalry, others that his partners wanted to keep him from talking. Another theory held that he was riling the other gang members by talking about retribution for their failure to pay for his friend McMahon's funeral. Either way, he never realized his agrarian ambitions of retiring to a quiet life on a farm.

It is also possible that an unrelated conflict led to Manning's killing. Clues about another side of Manning's criminal career emerged seventeen years later at a hearing on waterfront rack-eteering by the State Crime Commission. A waterfront gang-ster, Francis Smith, testified about how corrupt loading bosses controlled kickbacks and graft along the piers. Smith cited Manning as an example, identifying him as a member of the Rubel gang and a friend of Charlie Yanowsky of Jersey City, the waterfront racketeer who had become a longshoremen's union business agent. Smith testified that Manning wanted to grab the job of loading boss at Pier 90. (Whether this was before or after the Rubel robbery is unclear.) While Manning was rebuffed, he may have been killed by a rival gang faction in retaliation for trying, with Yanowsky, to take over territory in New York.

While some of the gang members went into hiding after the Rubel heist, Archie Stewart at first took the opposite tack. He immediately began making jaunts to Miami and Hot Springs, Arkansas, and reappearing at his old nightclub and burlesque haunts on Broadway on the theory that maintaining his usual routine would deflect police interest. He even caroused at a bar the same night that the FBI's J. Edgar Hoover had shown up there. One of Stewart's friends suggested he meet Hoover, but prudence got the better of him and he declined.

At other times, Stewart seemed to tempt fate. Twice in 1936 he was arrested in connection with other matters—once for an out-of-state warrant, then on a vagrancy charge. Each time he was questioned by a far higher-ranking officer than might be expected, namely John Ryan, the chief of detectives in Brooklyn. Both times he kept his counsel.

But his natural arrogance, and maybe also a need for cash, eventually got the better of him. He later testified that by the end of 1935, he had spent all his share of the Rubel loot. "I lived high, wide, and handsome," he said. With the money gone, he tried, and failed, at bookmaking.

So he and his fellow Rubel alumnus Stewart Wallace hooked up again, this time robbing a bank in Pine Bush, New York, in 1936. They took $14,000 and shot it out with the cops during a chase. Wallace took a round in the head, but he survived. Both men were convicted and sentenced to thirty to sixty years in prison, with Wallace sent to Auburn and Stewart to Clinton Prison in Dannemora, which was where Stewart crossed paths with Kress, the car thief, and tried to shake him down for money.

John Hughes, the boat owner, disappeared and was never heard from again.

The authorities arrested Francis Oley in Denver for the Albany kidnapping in January 1937 after the reader of a detective magazine identified him from a story about the case. He was extradited to New York and became the next of the Rubel gang to die. While being held at the jail in Oneida, he knotted strips of bed sheet, tied one end to the top of his cell door, and made a noose out of the other end for his neck. He stepped off his bunk into oblivion.

John Oley and Geary were now wanted for two major crimes: the O'Connell kidnapping and the Rubel robbery. Francis's arrest in the Albany case led to their downfall. One report at the time held that Francis's five-year-old daughter inadvertently revealed to authorities that John Oley had been writing letters to his brother, which led to the capture. But Francis himself may have betrayed his own brother. "He was a pisspot, a squealer," a source told William Kennedy in his Albany book. "They squeezed John's whereabouts out of him." Either way, on February 1, 1937, twelve days after Francis's arrest, federal agents and New York City police made raids in Brooklyn in connection with the O'Connell case.

The authorities surrounded a building on Bedford Avenue, where Geary was living in a fourth-floor apartment, and arrested him as he walked out of the front door, carrying a large quantity of money. Not a shot was fired. He was processed at the Snyder Avenue police station and taken to the federal lockup in Manhattan. Over at a building on St. Paul's Place, John Oley was asleep in blue pajamas in a back apartment on the fourth floor when he heard a knock on the door at about 2 a.m. Who was it, he demanded. "The superintendent," came the reply. Oley did not buy the subterfuge and began clambering onto the fire escape but gave up when he saw it being guarded by the police. Police found $750 in fifties and hundreds in his overcoat. Francis Phillips, the detective who had been helping lead the investigation, was there to see Oley in handcuffs.

The arrests of Geary and Oley were for the O'Connell case, but New York detectives were circling the two men like hawks for the Rubel heist. They were intent on questioning them. But federal authorities resisted, and William F. X. Geoghan, the Brooklyn district attorney, intervened to push the FBI to allow his investigators to proceed. William Lilienthal and John Wilson, two of the armored car guards, were brought in, but could not identify either man.

Meanwhile, the trial for the O'Connell kidnapping went ahead in United States District Court in Binghamton, New

York, and ended in convictions on August 12, 1937. Found guilty were Charles Harrigan, the Hoboken gangster enlisted to help with the kidnapping; four members of his crew; Manny Strewl; and Geary and John Oley. Three of the Hoboken gangsters were sent to Alcatraz, and another hanged himself in jail.

Oley and Geary were sentenced to seventy-seven years in prison. They and one of the convicted kidnappers, Harold Crowley, appealed, and were housed temporarily at the Onandaga County Penitentiary in Jamesville during the process. They did not stay in Jamesville for long.

On November 16, the three men escaped, led by Geary, who later told prison authorities at Leavenworth that he simply couldn't resist the temptation to run when the opportunity presented itself. As in the Rubel heist, Geary and Oley displayed a knack for planning and a flair for daring. Investigators later discovered that several bars in Oley's cell had been dislodged and held in place by chewing gum. They found that knives and files had been smuggled into the cellblock, along with two revolvers—a .38 Colt Bankers Special and a .38 Iver Johnson—possibly by Geary's wife. Geary, armed with the guns, walked out of his cell, crossed a corridor, and removed a bar that had also been cut from a cellblock anteroom. He opened a door, climbed a flight of stairs to another cell block, and hid behind a door.

When John Corbett, a guard, approached on his rounds, Geary jumped out, pointed a gun at him, and ordered him to ring the "all's well" bell. Geary hustled the guard to an office and ordered him to summon several other guards on duty, on the pretext that Oley was hanging himself. When they arrived, Geary marched the group to Oley's and Crowley's cells, forcing Corbett to open the doors. Geary snatched the keys from Corbett and relieved him of $35. The three prisoners tied up the guards with their neckties and belts, stuffed their mouths with mattress cotton, and put them in the cells the prisoners once occupied. When a guard named Nellie Hill stumbled upon the group, she too was grabbed and tied up.

Out in the prison yard, the three men ambushed another guard, Edward Hayes. They hustled him out to his car, grabbed the car keys, and bound him up too. But the car wouldn't start. They managed to get the vehicle running and drove five miles to Syracuse, with Hayes in the back seat and Geary next to him. At the prison, the guards struggled to free themselves; Hill managed to wriggle out of her bonds first. She quickly helped the others slip out of the ties and belts, and they called for help.

The men drove to the center of Syracuse, where they abandoned Hayes and his car, next stopping a driver, Henry King, and at gunpoint forcing him to take them toward Manlius, the very town near Syracuse where R. B. Davis had enlisted in the Union Army in another century. The prisoners knew how the police might react, including setting up roadblocks, and had second thoughts about traveling the main route. So they instructed King to take a side road and return to Syracuse, to his mother's house, where they ordered her to prepare them a meal. After they left, King told the police that the escapees had taken his overcoat and left one of theirs behind. The coat had belonged to John Corbett, the guard held in the jail break.

The police quickly traced Geary, Oley, and Crowley to a rooming house on the edge of Syracuse's downtown district. Their presence was revealed by a janitor, Ivan Whiteford, who was in the hallway of a vacant house looking at the place as a possible rental when the three escapees confronted him with guns. When they ordered him to help find them a room and food, he offered his own home. They agreed and the group motored to Whiteford's rooming house. He went out to procure food and liquor, came back, and drank with his unexpected guests to ingratiate himself with them. At the first opportunity, he slipped out to summon the police. When officers moved in for the arrests, on November 17, Crowley and Oley surrendered, but Geary escaped by jumping twenty feet out of a bathroom window, injuring his leg. The police found two revolvers stashed under a bed at the rooming house.

After their arrests, Oley and Crowley revealed that Geary had found a loose cell bar, removed it, and used chewing gum to hold it in place. They denied sawing the bar open, as it first seemed. "It was as easy as getting out of a paper bag," Oley explained. "These local cops are lots smarter than G-men. As for Geary, he's the smartest of all, but I imagine we'll be seeing him soon at Alcatraz."

The escape was splashy enough to land the convicts on *Gang Busters*, an immensely popular radio program of the era that reenacted police case histories. "Special flash! All citizens are asked to cooperate with the police in the apprehension of one of the most dangerous criminals at large today," the script read. "Percy Geary, 29, 5 feet 9½ inches tall, 134 pounds, chestnut hair, gray eyes. His two companions, Harold Crowley and John Oley, who escaped with him from Onondaga Penitentiary where they were serving terms for kidnapping, were captured today. But Geary escaped by jumping out of a window. He may be badly hurt, but should be approached with caution, as this man is desperate."

One of the listeners that evening was a parking lot attendant named Caspar Mirra, who worked near the rooming house where Oley and Crowley had been arrested. Shortly after the arrests, Mirra saw someone who looked like a bum sitting on a curb nearby. When the man said he had injured his foot tripping over a can, Mirra invited the unfortunate soul into a shack at the lot, where he warmed his hands in front of a stove in the corner.

Mirra connected his visitor to the *Gang Busters* report and told a customer of the parking lot to call the police. When an officer, his gun drawn, entered the shack, Percy Geary gave up without resistance. He was too weak to fight. Mirra received $2,000 in reward money, and Whiteford, the janitor whose tip led to the two arrests, took in $4,000. A week later, Agnes Oley and Josephine Geary, the wives of the two felons, were hauled in for harboring fugitives. They did not go as meekly as Geary, battling with police in a hair-pulling, clawing brawl. In a footnote, Mirra went on to get a job as a messenger at the Syracuse Savings Bank, where he deposited his reward money.

On January 26, 1938, John Oley and Percy Geary were convicted of the crime of escaping from the Onandaga jail. The jury deliberated for all of seventeen minutes before rendering their verdict. The defendants refused counsel and argued that they had been wrongly convicted in the O'Connell kidnapping, and so had a right to escape. The judge sentenced them to five additional years in prison.

Seven months later, on July 11, 1938, Geary and Oley finally arrived at Alcatraz to begin their seventy-seven-year prison terms for the O'Connell kidnapping. Hyman Barshay, the Rubel case prosecutor, later said he believed the two men used proceeds from the armored car robbery to help pay for their defense in the kidnapping trial.

Before his kidnappers went off to Alcatraz, Butch O'Connell, their victim, married Mary Fahey, the woman he had dated on the night of his kidnapping. Butch went on to serve as a figurehead leader of the Albany Democratic Committee, dying in 1954 at the age of forty-five.

CHAPTER 16.

No. 336: Rubber and Clay

THE SEVEN BEAUTIES REACHED THEIR FULL height of respectability with the arrival of the Penfields. They joined the Canavans, of the excavation business; the Takamines, of the biotech industry; the Davises, of the food industry; and the Fabers, pencil manufacturers. For the Penfields, prosperity derived from bricks and the machines that made them, which in turn created the materials that helped cities and towns grow across America.

After renting No. 336 in the years before World War I, the Penfields bought the townhouse in 1913. The family consisted of Raymond Penfield, his wife Minnie Patterson Penfield, their sons Harold Cassanove and James Preston, and their daughter Julia. Raymond Penfield was born in Willoughby, Ohio, on May 31, 1860. His grandfather founded the American Clay Machinery Co., a business that made bricks, clay-handling equipment, and tractors. After graduating from Wesleyan University in 1885, Raymond Penfield went right to work for the company. The sudden death of his father in the early 1890s thrust Raymond into the presidency of American Clay before he turned thirty. He adopted an aggressive strategy, acquiring control of the rival National Clay Manufacturing and the Great Eastern Clay Manufacturing companies. But it may have been the wrong move. Both were placed in receivership by 1903. In 1914, American Clay merged with the English company Hatfield to form the Hatfield-Penfield Steel Company, which adapted machinery once used by American Clay to make brick kilns for the manufacture of shells and other munitions for the Allied armies during World War I. The partnership dissolved after the war and Penfield retired in 1928.

While running American Clay, Penfield also served as president of two other companies: the American Equipment Company of Chicago, which he helped found, and more notably, starting in 1898, the Goodyear Tire and Rubber Company. He was Goodyear's second president, and presumably benefited from family connections: Frank A. Seiberling, who founded the tiremaker, was married to Penfield's sister Gertrude.

Penfield's other mark on turn-of-the-century business history in America was the invention of a new mechanical system to handle bricks during their production. In 1918, with the end of his wartime munitions endeavor, Penfield set up the New York Brickhandling Corp. in 1918 to put the system to use, and ran the company for ten years. Penfield had some sort of crisis in this period because the *Herald-Tribune*, in its obituary, said he "suffered a nervous breakdown" soon after the war and never fully recovered. But the war was good for him economically.

During their time on Riverside Drive, the Penfields' twenty-room elevator-equipped home played host to parties, receptions, concerts, and a celebration of their silver wedding anniversary on May 27, 1910. The contralto Beatrice McCue, accompanied by the violinist Roland Meyer, gave a recital on a winter Friday afternoon in 1912. One of the most lavish events of all was the reception after a double wedding for Harold and Julia, herself a singer, on June 19, 1912, at St. Paul's Methodist Episcopal Church on West End Avenue and 86th Street.

The wedding was the sort of grand affair that received prominent coverage in the newspapers. Both couples entered the church simultaneously and processed down separate aisles under arches of pink roses. Julia, who was marrying Aaron Bastedo, a fellow singer, wore a coronet of orange blossoms and a diamond necklace and held a bouquet of orchids and lilies of the valley. Her cousin, Irene Seiberling, was the maid of honor. Harold married Anna Bullwinkel, a Brooklyn girl.

The 1930 census put the Penfield house's value at $98,000. The family, who were attended to by their African American butler, Harry Campbell, also had a renter, a raincoat salesman named Rufus Hubbard, who paid $75 a month for lodging. Were the Penfields in financial need? Maybe they were acting altruistically. Hubbard was a World War I veteran.

Penfield died of pneumonia in 1932, and seventy-five people gathered at No. 336 for his funeral. He was seventy-two and had been weakened from a fractured shoulder suffered in a fall as he headed down train steps in Rye, New York. Hymns filled the halls: "Face to Face," "There is No Death," "The Lord's Prayer," and "Lead, Kindly Light." An old Wesleyan classmate, the Reverend Francis Upham, helped officiate. Penfield was buried in the village cemetery of Willoughby, Ohio, the town where he was born.

The Penfield family story gives some insight into the changing fortunes of Riverside Drive, which never really lived up to its promise as a new Fifth Avenue. Within their first thirty-five years of life, our row of townhouses began showing decay. Tully's establishment, two doors down from the Penfields, was a pretty clear sign. Just two blocks north on Riverside was another establishment dedicated to sin, and one that drew the crusading energies of Minnie Penfield, the matriarch of No. 336. Minnie joined her neighbors in fighting to close the establishment, which was grandly but incongruously named the Patrician and played host to weddings, dances, and private parties. A lawyer for the neighbors, John Sullivan, said the owners of the Patrician would hold any sort of event for money. "One can hear the blare of jazz music there every night," he harrumphed at a hearing before the city's Board of Standards and Appeals. "Taxicabs congregate about the place at all hours and men and women revelers stand and sit about on the steps and talk loudly until the very late hours. I would not go so far as to say there is drinking there, but the noise is very disconcerting to the residents of the neighborhood." The board ordered the place shut. The fight between neighbors and noise-generating establishments is an age-old one in New York City.

Indeed, the whole area of the Upper West Side, especially in the side streets between the grand avenues of West End, Broadway, Central Park West, and Riverside Drive, developed a seedier aspect after the initial development rush at the beginning of the twentieth century. Pigeon coops came to dot rooftops— the gang lord Owney Madden even had one atop the majestic Belnord apartment house on 86th Street and Broadway. Away from the elegant residential avenues, street urchins plucked cigarette butts from the sidewalk and populated crap games. Speakeasies, gambling parlors, and bordellos sprouted in the neighborhood, mostly in side-street tenements. Shantytowns, many inhabited by World War I veterans, arose near the shores of the Hudson River during the Depression. Bars filled buckets with beer, called growlers, for local patrons. Bonfires would roar on election day. The Depression was taking its toll.

The novelist James Salter, in his lyrical memoir *Burning the Days: Recollection*, captures the texture of life on the Upper West Side in the 1930s. Born in 1925, Salter lived on West End Avenue as a boy. "In the city that first took shape for me there were large apartment buildings stretching as far as one could see in either direction. On the side streets were private houses, many of which had been divided into rooms. Along Riverside Drive stood unspoiled mansions, stranded, as if waiting for aged patriarchs to die."

He continues: "In the bleak back courtyards men with grinding wheels sometimes still appeared, ringing a bell and calling up to housewives or kitchen maids for knives and scissors to sharpen." (In 2017, a knife-grinding truck would still pass through the streets, alerting residents with a ringing bell.) "Nature meant the trees and narrow park along the river, and perhaps one of the rare snowstorms, with traffic in the streets dying and the silence of the world wrapping around. Newsboys, so-called though they were men, often walked along late in the day shouting something over and over, *Extra! Extra!*, someone murdered, something collapsed or sunk."

This was the world of the Penfield clan, and the younger children reflected the contradictory quality of the neighborhood. To their disgrace, this upright family soon had something in common with McMahon, Manning, and company: arrest records. Two grandchildren of the Penfield patriarch, the second president of Goodyear tire, turned to petty crime. Marguerite Penfield, the teenage daughter of Harold and Anna, and granddaughter of Raymond Penfield, was arrested in 1930 for stealing two bottles of perfume, worth $25, from Macy's while she was visiting from Chicago. She said she wanted to give them as Christmas presents to her aunt, the wife of James Penfield. (James and his wife were living at No. 336 at the time.) Marguerite told the judge that her grandmother did not give her money to buy presents and that she stole the perfume on impulse. The charges were dismissed.

John Bastedo, another grandson and the son of Aaron and Julia, became a more ambitious thief. He began his criminal career at sixteen in 1936 in California, with auto theft, and was later arrested for burglary in Schoharie County, near Albany. In 1939, while living in Long Island City, Queens, he was charged with stealing cash, securities, and jewelry worth $5,000 from his grandmother during visits to No. 336. He pleaded guilty to grand larceny. A few months later, he was placed on probation for stealing another $6,500 worth of his grandmother's jewelry. In July 1940, Bastedo pleaded guilty to forging his grandmother's signature on two checks, for $150 and $50. Grandma Minnie had a soft spot for John. It must have been wrenching to be victimized by a beloved grandson, and one wonders about the kinds of excuses he offered her. Despite the forged checks, the stolen money, and the lifted jewels, she pleaded for mercy for her twenty-year-old grandson. But it was to no avail. The judge sent Bastedo to the Elmira Reformatory, the alma mater of Bernard McMahon, who six years earlier had died two doors away from Bastedo's grandmother's house.

CHAPTER 17.

Breakthrough

A T THE BEGINNING OF FEBRUARY 1937, two key members of the Rubel robbery team, John Oley and Percy Geary, were under arrest—charged with the O'Connell kidnapping, not the robbery. They refused to cooperate with New York City detectives pressing them for details on the heist. But prosecutors had another route: Thomas Quinn, the boatman. It had been a struggle. First Quinn admitted owning the getaway boats, but denied knowing they were used in a crime. Then he acknowledged being aware they were to be used in some sort of criminal caper, but said he was not involved. Finally, probably confronted with witnesses who put him in John Oley's company, he went a step further, admitting that the Oley brothers had used one of his boats in the heist.

On February 3, the Brooklyn district attorney, William Geoghan, revealed some details. Quinn claimed he took the boat out on the day in question from West 96th Street for a fishing trip with two men he did not know. He headed south on the Hudson River to 48th Street, tied up, and went to eat at a lunch cart while waiting to pick up several other individuals. When he came back, Quinn said, his passengers and boat were gone. Using photographs supplied by the police, he identified the two men as the Oley brothers. That was enough for Geoghan to present evidence to a Kings County grand jury naming John Oley as a perpetrator in the Rubel case.

But prosecutors needed more. Oley and Geary were ensconced in Alcatraz, and with Manning, McMahon, and Francis Oley dead, Hughes missing, and Wallace in prison, investigators turned to one of their last options: Archie Stewart, who was imprisoned at Dannemora. John Ryan, the Brooklyn chief of detectives who had already questioned Stewart on previous occasions, and Francis Madden, an assistant district attorney and top deputy in the Brooklyn District Attorney's office, spent four days in the summer of 1937 up at the prison trying to pry information out of him. They had no success. Then the warden and state corrections commissioner took a crack at Stewart—again without results. But a tiny opening had appeared from a surprising source.

The Bronx District Attorney's office, for unrelated reasons, had brought an inmate from Dannemora down to the city and during questioning seized on a bit of information from the man: it seemed that Archie Stewart had a younger brother named Robert who had decided to take his life in a different direction. He was a probationary police officer in New York. It was the perfect opportunity. Investigators approached Robert, who pronounced himself willing to help. What motivated Robert? Was he the kind of guy able to sell out his own brother for the sake of ambition, as a way of currying favor to rise in the police force? Was he truly an upright future cop who believed that justice should trump blood ties? Did he know the best chance for his brother was to cut a deal? That latter is more likely, given evidence that emerged later showing Robert's efforts to help out his sibling.

Whatever Robert's motives, the investigators sent him up to Dannemora to work on his brother Archie. His efforts were met, at first, with disdain. Archie had no inclination to help his brother further the cause of law enforcement. Robert kept at it, stressing the shame Archie had brought on their family. Eventually, Robert must have said something that worked. After three days, Archie agreed to talk. (Robert later became a full police officer and was soon promoted to detective.)

The case was cracked. On October 13, 1938, Archie Stewart was brought to Brooklyn and testified before a grand jury. He identified the gang at the Rubel Ice Company as himself, Kress, Wallace, the Oleys, Geary, Quinn, Hughes, Manning, and McMahon. Stewart later retraced the crime scenes with the detectives and identified the recovered boats and the pushcart.

The whole story spilled out. According to Stewart, who somewhat grandiosely placed himself at the center of the narrative, he was the crime's mastermind: he claimed to have come up with the idea for the robbery in June of 1934 and picked each new member of the gang. He planned the robbery, which was sketched out over nine separate meetings. He gave each member of the gang a task. He divvied up the proceeds. McMahon and Manning chose Kress, Stewart would later testify, to provide the two stolen cars. Kress drove one of them on the day of the robbery, he said. McMahon drove the other car. Hughes piloted the speedboat and Quinn handled the lobster boat.

Distancing himself from a potential gun charge, Stewart laid the responsibility for providing the weapons on Manning and McMahon—Manning the pistols and McMahon the machine guns. McMahon also made the initial contact with Hughes, for the boats, and Hughes brought Quinn into the affair. This was all according to Stewart, who was clearly looking for a deal with prosecutors by trading on his inside knowledge of the crime.

Stewart also suggested that investigators pay a call to John Oley and Percy Geary at Alcatraz. In October 1938, the relentless Ryan and Madden met with the two men. With nothing to lose, the convicts gave information implicating Gilbert, the doctor called to treat McMahon, and Quinn, the boat owner. Within short order, Gilbert was picked up and held on $50,000 bail. An affidavit described McMahon's death from gangrene and infection, along with Gilbert's role in helping cut off McMahon's legs so his body could be stuffed into a trunk.

Police quickly grabbed Madeline Tully, the rooming house doyenne, hauling her out of a dingy walk-up apartment in Yorkville, on Manhattan's far East Side. Just a few weeks earlier, Tully had finished serving a thirty-month sentence in connection with a raid on a rooming house she ran at 322 West 90th Street.

That raid gives a clear picture of the level of trust the underworld placed in Tully, and of her formidable criminal ties. Police at 90th Street arrested nine members of what was dubbed the Arsenal Gang and seized a sizable cache of firearms. It also serves as a reminder of the Upper West Side's occasional violent history. The house on 90th Street, which was used as a hideaway and headquarters, sat just a few doors down from the building where police had carried out the notorious siege of Francis "Two-Gun" Crowley, who for a brief time in the early '30s was considered the most dangerous man in New York. One of those arrested during the raid on Tully's building was Albert Ackalitis, a West Side gangster and future waterfront crime boss who would one day rule Pier 18 and, from there, parts of the Hudson County docks across the river. It was believed that the Arsenal Gang's leader was another criminal boss on the docks, Frank Peraski, a member of the Yanowsky crime faction that included Manning and McMahon. The arrests of Ackalitis and Peraski demonstrate the close links between organized crime rings that operated throughout the city and the world of kickbacks, loansharking, illegal betting, and murder on the docks.

Tully appeared in court in Brooklyn on October 22, 1938 and was charged as a material witness in the Rubel case. Madden, the assistant DA, told the judge that Tully lived in the apartment where McMahon had been brought and later died. Madden asked for the same bail for Tully as for Dr. Gilbert, $50,000. But the judge, John Fitzgerald, set the amount at $15,000, ruling that Tully—despite her underworld bona fides—wasn't "in the same class" as Gilbert. She was taken to the so-called "civil jail" next to the Raymond Street lockup in what is now Fort Greene, Brooklyn.

On a cloudy November 3, 1938, the indictment in the Rubel case was handed up. The *Brooklyn Eagle* gave it a banner headline: 9 INDICTED FOR RUBEL ROBBERY. Tully and Gilbert were named as accessories and seven others as participants: Wallace, Stewart, Kress, Quinn, John Oley, Geary, and Hughes. But only three members of the gang of ten would actually be tried: Kress, one of the two drivers, who was already in jail on a gun charge; Wallace, who was also in jail, for a bank robbery; and Quinn, the boatman. Three others were dead: McMahon, the victim of the self-inflicted shotgun wound; Manning, felled by a gunman on an upper Manhattan sidewalk; and Francis Oley, who had hanged himself at the Oneida jail. Hughes was missing. Oley and Geary, the former rumrunners and kidnappers from Albany, were in federal prison. Stewart was to become the state's key witness.

The prosecution was assigned to Hyman Barshay, a tailor's son born in Russia who came to the United States at the age of seven. Growing up in Williamsburg, Brooklyn, then a major destination for the city's immigrant Jews, Barshay sold newspapers to earn money in high school, and from there went straight to Brooklyn Law school at night, working various jobs during the day. A brilliant young man, he graduated at the age of twenty and immediately landed in the prosecutor's office. Barshay had an aloof, even severe character. Years after the Rubel case, Barshay was appointed as a judge on the state Supreme Court, where he was a stern presence.

At the time Barshay took over the case, the Brooklyn District Attorney's office was not considered a stellar example of prosecutorial skill. Geoghan, the DA, was a Philadelphia-born lawyer who moved to New York in 1906 and taught high school and college English. Four years later, he went into private practice, then served as an assistant district attorney and ran for Congress as a Democrat in 1921, losing amid a Republican landslide. Geoghan's honesty and loyalty to the Democratic machine were unquestioned. His competency as a crimefighter was another story. In 1935, the body of Samuel Drukman, a racetrack gambler and mechanic, was found in a car trunk at the Luckman Brothers Garage in Brooklyn. He had been beaten with a billiard cue and strangled. Two suspects were found in the garage, and they conveniently had blood on their clothes. A third suspect, the company's owner, Meyer Luckman (father of the future football star Sid Luckman), was arrested outside.

Yet Geoghan's office failed to win an indictment. State hearings on Geoghan's removal followed, along with allegations that officials had been bribed to undermine the case. Governor Herbert H. Lehman, a Democrat, eventually absolved Geoghan of all charges, declaring him "an honest man." But in an indirectly stinging rebuke to Geoghan, Lehman appointed a special prosecutor, Hiram Todd, to handle the Drukman case. The suspects were eventually convicted of second degree murder.

In 1939 Lehman appointed another special prosecutor, John Harlan Amen, to investigate official corruption in Brooklyn. One of Amen's targets was Francis Madden, Geoghan's top deputy and close friend, who was eventually convicted of taking bribes to protect an illegal abortion enterprise and was later disbarred.

Stewart Wallace's lawyer was Burton Turkus, a man described as "suave, dynamic in conversation, sharp," by the Associated Press reporter Sid Feder in the introduction to *Murder, Inc.: The Story of the Syndicate*, a book he and Turkus co-wrote about the notorious killing organization. Despite Feder's description of his co-writer as a political independent, Turkus was politically connected and on the rise—a prominent Democrat in Brooklyn whose name was tossed around as a potential United States attorney, a member of the Elks and Knights of Pythias and various other clubs and lawyers' organizations. He showed up frequently in the pages of newspapers, standing demurely behind or next to a happy client, wearing a homburg and pocket square in his buttoned suit jacket, his mustache trimmed into a flattened triangle. Turkus carved out a reputation as a divorce lawyer in the 1920s, often representing the aggrieved wife in cases, covered avidly by the papers, involving attempted poisonings, love triangles, and best-friend betrayals. It was perhaps the closest genre of that era to reality TV and *Real Housewives* dramas.

In another noteworthy case, Turkus represented Helen Walsh, the girlfriend of Francis "Two-Gun" Crowley, in her efforts to see the convicted killer on the eve of his execution at Sing Sing in 1932. Crowley refused to receive the young woman, who was arrested with him during the 90th Street siege—witnessed by scores of people filling the streets. She just wanted to sell her story to the papers, he said. "To hell with her," prison officials quoted him as saying. Turkus also fought to dismiss an all-white jury about to hear a murder case against two black men—the first instance of challenging a jury's racial composition in New York State, according to the *Brooklyn Eagle*. The case was rendered moot when the two men pleaded guilty. But the judge in the case—O'Dwyer—called on Turkus to submit his arguments anyway. It would not be the last time that O'Dwyer demonstrated his respect for the lawyer.

In *Murder, Inc.*, Turkus explained how he came to be involved in the Rubel case. One day, O'Dwyer, who was to be the judge at the trial, buttonholed Turkus outside the Brooklyn criminal court building. "He turned on the irresistible charm which has been the man's most remarkable asset as a public figure," Turkus wrote. "'I wish you would take the defense of this man Wallace,'" the judge told him. Turkus was reluctant. He was swamped with cases and "this had all the earmarks of a long drawn-out trial." Turkus continued: "Besides, although no lawyer has the right to prejudge guilt, it is only human, at times, to sense no real defense. This case had exactly that flavor." So he told O'Dwyer he'd rather decline. The judge countered with flattery: Wallace deserved a good lawyer, one as good as the top representatives that the other defendants had. "That was the O'Dwyer charm at work. Few have been able to resist it," Turkus noted.

Kress, the car thief, was represented at first by Sam Leibowitz, a celebrated criminal lawyer, and later by Vincent Impellitteri, who would go on to serve as mayor of New York City from 1950 to 1953. Quinn had Caesar Barra as his courtroom defender.

Even though the police were confident that they had solved the case, the prosecution wanted more insider witnesses to ensure convictions. Brooklyn investigators traveled once again to Alcatraz, to try to persuade Oley and Geary to testify, but they refused. So they had to rely on Archie Stewart, who agreed to testify against his former co-conspirators in return for immunity. His residence did not change: Clinton Prison in Dannemora, where he was serving that thirty- to sixty-year sentence for the bank robbery committed with Wallace in Pine Bush, New York. Stewart was seeking leniency regarding his conviction for the bank robbery, and may also have been motivated by revenge. He bore a grudge against Kress.

On June 26, 1939, just short of five years after the robbery, the lawyers and three defendants appeared at the Kings County Courthouse for jury selection. The building, a neoclassical pile on Joralemon and Fulton Streets in downtown Brooklyn, was considered in desperate need of repair and improvements. But outside it was a glory of tall arches, pediments, and an imposing dome, all to be torn down in the following decade to make way for a modern civic complex. Inside the courtroom, tension was high. More than a dozen detectives carefully scrutinized the spectators' gallery.

In his opening argument, Barshay described the case in stark terms. "I shall prove that each of the participants was assigned to a specific role," the prosecutor told the jurors. "It was agreed that they were to apply Newskin to their fingertips to avoid leaving fingerprints, that each was to be unshaven for a few days prior to the crime, that each was to be dressed to appear like the workmen who congregate in front of the Rubel plant, that each was to wear smoked glasses and caps, that each was to hire a pushcart similar to those used by the peddlers and to present himself with his cart in the neighborhood of the plant on several days before the day of the robbery so their faces would not appear strange and arouse suspicion." And he went on to say, "I shall prove that the plan was often rehearsed prior to its actual execution."

The first witnesses to take the stand were bank officials, who testified about the sums of money that were carried by the armored car, and explained that the cash became US Trucking's responsibility once in the car's care. Lilienthal, one of the guards, despite the bitterness over his treatment by the armored car company, then took the stand and described the robbery but insisted that he could not recognize the three defendants. Conveniently, the one gang member he said he did recognize was not on trial. That would be Archie Stewart.

Stewart was the star witness, repeating the account he had given to the grand jury. He said he was with McMahon and Manning in June 1934 when they saw the armored car in Coney Island that served as their inspiration, adding, "We decided it would be an easy job to take over." To trace the movements of the gang members, he used a six-by-four-foot blown-up photograph, with each player represented by a white square of paper pinned to the picture. Stewart testified that Kress took part in the robbery and received a $47,000 cut of the proceeds, the same amount as the other principals. Quinn and Hughes, Stewart said, produced and operated the boats used in the getaway, so each pocketed a half-share for their efforts. Wallace also received a half-share because with only one hand, he was considered half as effective. He did not explain what happened to the other half.

Charles Schlayer, a mechanic, testified that he repaired the speedboat used in the robbery and that Hughes, John Oley, Stewart, and Kress took the craft out for a jaunt in the Hudson River, a trip which the prosecution described as a test run. Schlayer said he remembered this event clearly because guards at the dock of a Ford plant in Edgewater, New Jersey, a narrow strip of town across the river from a stretch of Manhattan extending from about 96th Street to 170th Street, refused to let the men land.

The defense countered by putting a Ford personnel manager on the stand to undercut the mechanic's testimony. The manager testified that no armed guards were present at the plant that year. Quinn's lawyer called to the stand three longshoremen, associates of his client, to say that on the day of the robbery he was hanging out on the street or in a saloon from 11:30 a.m. to 1 p.m. in Manhattan's "stovepipe" section, as the area just north of Hell's Kitchen was then known. Quinn's lawyer also tried to cast aspersions on the credibility of Stewart's brother, the police officer, by seeking to introduce Dictaphone recordings. The recordings depicted a conversation between the patrolman and two longshoremen bosses. Presumably, the recordings would have shown some sort of involvement by the officer in illegal waterfront activity.

Stewart testified that he and Kress had met again in Sing Sing in 1937, where Kress was serving his sentence for gun possession and where he was still incarcerated at the time of the trial. Stewart said he demanded $500 more for McMahon's medical treatment and burial, and that Kress gave him only $150. Stewart said Kress promised to come up with more, although how much more is unknown. But whatever the amount, it was enough for Stewart to keep after Kress. He asked several times for the rest of the money, with no success. Was the money really payback for McMahon's treatment and burial? It may have been a shakedown, funds extorted with the threat that Stewart would do just what he was engaged in: implicating Kress in the Rubel crime.

But Stewart was also running out of money to pay his lawyers and cover the cost of printing legal documents. "I need the money you owe me," he told Kress. Kress agreed to pay him through his brother-in-law, Harold Harkavy, a lawyer. Who could fetch the money, he asked Stewart. Stewart said he would send his brother Robert, the police officer who served as the middleman with prosecutors. Robert failed to procure the cash and Stewart went back to Dannemora. The matter was dropped.

In his testimony, Kress denied most of the allegations against him regarding Stewart's demands, and offered a different version of his contacts with Stewart in prison. Kress testified that one day he told some fellow inmates that he had a lawyer brother-in-law who was looking into his appeal. Stewart overheard the conversation, Kress continued, said he was interested in using him, and asked for his name and address.

To explain his connection to the robbery charges, Kress came up with a rather flimsy story. He claimed that Stewart effectively threatened to implicate him unless he was paid to stay quiet. Here is Kress quoting Stewart: "Listen Kress, I have a very expensive lawyer handling my appeal, and I need dough. I don't care where or how I get it. I got my brother hustling all over New York, but I don't care how or where he gets it either. I want you to kick back that dough or else it will be just too bad for you." And here is where Kress cast himself in an innocent light, complaining that he "never received a nickel from anybody for that." And Stewart wouldn't receive a cent from him.

Kress's lawyer called Harkavy to the stand to back up his client. Harkavy described a series of encounters with Robert Stewart and growing demands for money. "You know it would be rather unhealthy for Joe if a contribution was not made," Harkavy quoted Robert Stewart as saying. "Archie could make it pretty hot for Joe, make things very uncomfortable for Joe." Harkavy resisted but finally caved. "Your threat worked and has scared Joe's mother to such an extent that he has given me—Joe's father has given me some money for you," Harkavy testified.

When Quinn and Kress took the stand, both denied outright taking part in the robbery. Kress also specified that he had no involvement in any planning, the getaway, or division of the loot and did not even know the other gang members. He denied seeing Schlayer, the mechanic who was said to have repaired the speedboat. He did, however, admit to something else: being a loser. He called himself "a loafer and a gambler and the black sheep of my family."

In his summation, Barshay called the heist "the crime of the century." Like a good trial lawyer, he anticipated the defense's closing statements by saying that his case involved no exaggeration and lacked "phony witnesses." By that he meant witnesses who did not know what they were talking about because they were not there. Stewart had been—and though no choir boy, he was eminently well placed to give the inside story. Barshay spoke for two hours, ending at 10:30 p.m., at which point O'Dwyer adjourned the trial until 10 the next morning.

On the day of defense summations, the lawyers managed to shave away some aspects of the case, persuading O'Dwyer to dismiss the charges of assault and grand larceny. The jury would now have to decide only on first-degree robbery charges.

In their closing arguments, the defense employed a time-tested strategy: kill the messenger. They argued that Archie Stewart, the insider who had provided the bulk of the evidence against their clients, was actually the guilty party—guilty, they argued, of manufacturing a plot to implicate the defendants.

"Archie Stewart is a human cobra if ever I saw one," Turkus railed. "Archie Stewart tells you that his only motive in testifying in this trial is to gain immunity from prosecution for participating in the Rubel job. You can't believe that. His motive is to gain his release from the sentence of thirty to sixty years he is serving in Dannemora prison for his part in the Pine Bush National Bank robbery.

"If you want to pull the chestnuts out of the fire for him and send him back on the public with a gun in his hands, go ahead and convict three suckers who are defendants in this case. Stewart Wallace, my client, is an old man with only one hand. He could have made the same deal. He could have made a deal to put Kress and Quinn in jail to save his own skin. But he wouldn't do it. He wouldn't tell lies to put the finger on others."

Indeed, the Court of Appeals would later cast doubt on Archie Stewart's account, saying there were "contradictions and improbabilities in his testimony and it did not always square with other established facts." His veracity, the court added, "was open to the gravest suspicion." Turkus, in cross-examining him, at one point sought to undermine his credibility by connecting him to unrelated killings. Specifically, Turkus asked Stewart if he was responsible for the murder of one John (Ky) Costello in Manhattan, a crime that had not been solved. No, Stewart replied, he was not. It was a line of questioning insisted on by Wallace. He had gone so far as to tell O'Dwyer he would represent himself if those questions were not asked.

The case went to the jury at midday on July 12. Because Judge O'Dwyer had dismissed the grand larceny and assault charges, the jurors had a simple choice to make: conviction or acquittal on one count of first-degree robbery for each defendant. On the first afternoon of deliberations, the jurors asked to re-hear portions of testimony. Dinner arrived at 7:45 p.m., and within an hour and fifteen minutes, they were back at work.

The night dragged on. At 3 a.m., the verdict came back for all three defendants: guilty. When the verdict was announced, none of them displayed any reaction. In explaining the verdict later, Wallace's lawyer, Turkus, said the defense had little room to maneuver: "The state had too many loaded guns," he wrote in *Murder, Inc.* The verdict was cast as proof that no crime, no matter how minutely planned, was immune from discovery. On its editorial page, the *Brooklyn Eagle* opined: "That the long arm of the law was able to strike so effectively, even after the passage of nearly five years, demonstrated once more that the cleverest of crooks are unable to plan and execute a really perfect crime."

When sentencing time came, Wallace could have gotten up to sixty years as a second-time offender, but O'Dwyer gave him thirty years, and made the term run concurrent to the thirty years Wallace was already serving for the bank robbery. Kress and Quinn faced the same maximum, but received a ten- to thirty-year sentence.

At sentencing, Wallace demonstrated a burst of altruism and sought to clear his co-defendants, declaring that while he may have been guilty, they took no part in the robbery. "I want to make a statement," he said. "I'm guilty of this crime, but these two men are not. For the record, I want to state that there were not ten men involved but only nine and these men are not two of the nine men who committed this crime."

Lawyers for Kress and Quinn jumped on the statement, and asked O'Dwyer to keep their clients in the city jail system, in Brooklyn, for forty-eight hours before ordering their transfer to a state prison. That would give them time, they said, to file a motion for a new trial based on new evidence. But the judge turned them down, saying the matter was up to the Department of Corrections. He said he did not want to take responsibility for sending the men to the Brooklyn jail, especially since it had taken on a porous quality: two inmates had escaped the previous week.

O'Dwyer, the future crusading prosecutor, also did something that these days would be unheard of in a criminal trial. He called the prosecutor, Barshay, and Ryan, the police inspector, up to the bench to deliver his congratulations. The money, all $427,950 of it, had disappeared.

CHAPTER 18.

No. 337:
Miss Havisham's House

Within a quarter of an hour we came to Miss Havisham's House,
which was of old brick, and dismal, and had a great many iron bars
to it.

—*Great Expectations*, by Charles Dickens

FOR A READER OF DICKENS'S NOVEL *Great Expectations*, the
melancholy weirdness of Satis House, the mysterious mansion where the corpse-like Miss Havisham, living in a state of
suspended imagination, receives Pip, is unforgettable. I was a
serious Dickens reader in my teen and college years, and somehow I transferred my idea of Satis House to a nearby building
that had been part of my own childhood, though not to Pip's
extent. It was on my corner growing up and it is another palazzo
with a name, River Mansion. The address is 337 Riverside
Drive.

Compared to the limestone Beaux-Arts airiness of its sisters
to the south, No. 337 gives off a lonelier air, with its red brick
facade and scraggly bushes behind metal fences. Ornate columns
reminiscent of the medieval Cloisters up the Hudson flank the

main entrance facing 106th Street. The columns are topped by a small stone porch set in front of a window, crowned by a cornice with lion heads on the brackets. A stone framework rises up two stories above the first floor, uniting two floors' worth of windows to the left and right side. The stonework is weighty. Limestone adornments stand in contrast to the wine-red brick.

By 1909, River Mansion had passed to Matilda Brower, a widow, whose household included a daughter, a son and his wife, two grandchildren, three Finnish servants, and an English nurse. The next recorded residents were the family of the businessman John McKinnon, who in September 1914 announced that his daughters Lillian Clare and Madeleine Agnes were engaged. Lillian was getting married to the melodiously named Maltby Jelliffe of Jersey City, and Madeleine found her match across the street: Kenneth Marwin of 340 Riverside Drive. How convenient Riverside Park would have been for the two couples. I imagine Maltby coming to town by ferry and hiring a car to head north, meeting Lillian, her sister, and Kenneth under the Franz Sigel statue. I see each strolling arm in arm, one pair in front of the other, a happy quartet out for warm evening walks in the summer before the start of World War I, discussing their weddings.

Within months of the engagements, a man named Charles Barkley bought the house and flipped it to another buyer. Three investors bought the building in 1921. Somehow life at No. 337 never settled down in the early years. It changed hands the most among the Seven Beauties.

Count Carl Armfelt, a former diplomat, arrived from Copenhagen with his new bride to take up occupancy at River Mansion in 1923. "I have a family which I can trace back for 500 years, but I want to work, and that is the reason

I have come to America," Armfelt told the *Times*. The ship that brought him, the *Frederick VIII*, also carried 200 Swedish and Danish immigrants planning to settle on farmland in the Northwest.

During the 1920s, the mansion continued to find new owners. Even before the Depression, when single-family homes began breaking up more and more, River Mansion had almost certainly become a boardinghouse, and a 1937 certificate of occupancy made it officially a purveyor of furnished rooms. Throughout the autumn of 1930, a resident named Madame Bittain advertised her services: the restoration of "old, faded or discolored tapestries." In the summer of 1935, a doctor named William J. Spring, an immigrant from Dresden, Germany, who earned his medical degree at Columbia University, lived there in a fourth-floor apartment with his wife Lila and fifteen-month-old child. Spring jumped to his death from an empty apartment above. He had been depressed, his wife said, and a terrible heat wave had apparently worn his nerves ragged to the breaking point.

Living in another room in the house at the time was Michael De Santis, a forty-three-year-old Italian immigrant who had studied art in Naples. By the early 1920s, De Santis was working as a commercial artist and became one of the first tenants of the Masters Apartment building at Riverside Drive and 103rd Street, paying $70 a month in 1930 to live in the just-constructed Art Deco skyscraper, built to house the museum and institute dedicated to the work of the artist and theosophist Nicholas Roerich. Roerich was a famous and powerful painter who had designed the sets for Stravinsky's *Rite of Spring* and had wealthy backers for his global travels and multidisciplinary school, the Master Institute of United Arts. Maybe De Santis felt at home in the company of a great artistic spirit, or maybe he felt frustrated by the limitations of his newfound specialty: academic portraits. De Santis made it his métier in the later 1920s, usually painting the scholars from likenesses after they died, and often rendering their wives too. The Massachusetts Institute of Technology, Union College, and the University of Rochester were said to own his works. Not surprisingly, professors at Columbia University, just a half-mile to the north of De Santis's final home, were a major source of patronage.

De Santis painted at least one Columbia personage a year from 1929 to 1935. But commissions were small and not frequent enough, and De Santis's fortunes declined. He was forced to leave the Masters and rented a studio apartment in a Columbia University building on 115th Street in 1932. He continued to struggle, and resorted to pleading for help from none other than Nicholas Butler, the towering president of Columbia, who had won the Nobel Peace Prize two years earlier. De Santis might have been encouraged by a signed note from Butler acknowledging receipt of a portrait of the Columbia professor Henry Drisler. Butler called it an "admirable representation of one of our fine old Columbia scholars of a past generation."

Five weeks after the acknowledgment, De Santis issued his painfully obsequious plea for financial help. He starts out by saying how much talent and training he has poured into the portraits he has done for Columbia. "In all of this work I have given most of my time to keep up the standard of good work and for your Institution's sake," he wrote, and then noted that he accepted payments below market rate. (The Drisler painting brought him $150.) "It has been almost impossible to meet my obligations fully," he lamented. And now, trouble loomed. He had fallen woefully behind in rent at his studio at 115th Street, in the Columbia building. The rental agents let him slide for a while. But their patience had run out. Now, he wrote, they want "to put me out on the street."

"I am very much grieved and in distress over the matter," he continued. "My dear Sir, I beg your forgiveness for bringing this matter to you, but if there is anything possible for an adjustment I shall be very grateful."

His appeal failed. Two days later, a secretary to Butler passed on the president's sympathies, along with a bureaucratic dodge. "Unfortunately, however, he has no practical suggestion to make." The treasurer and finance committee controlled the university's funds "and there is nothing that any of the rest of us can do in connection with them. The president is very sorry not to be able to make a more helpful reply." Soon after, De Santis moved to his room at 337 Riverside Drive.

Within four months of the letter, De Santis found himself at Bellevue Hospital and after a month and a half there, he was dead of a brain tumor, destitute. Fellow artists arranged a sale of 100 oil paintings, watercolors, and pastels by their colleague to pay for his funeral. One image was some sort of allegorical canvas painted originally as a gift for President Franklin D. Roosevelt. The works went on view at the Toran Decorative Art Studios, a collective display space created for indigent artists. The founder, Alphonse T. Toran, told the *Herald-Tribune*, "I can assure you, the paintings are excellent and it's enough if they bring $3 or $4 apiece."

De Santis was survived by his parents, Nicholas and Rosa, of the Bronx, and his brothers Ralph, Joseph, James, Dominick, and Carmine and sisters Rose, Mary, Anna, and Concetta. This last was the only one of the siblings who had a job, the newspaper said, also pointing out that two family members were "on relief," a small-hearted reference in the man's obituary. De Santis's funeral was held at Holy Name Roman

Catholic Church at 96th Street in Manhattan, ten blocks from his room. He was buried at St. Raymond's Cemetery in the Bronx.

These are the bare facts of the life of an obscure artist who arrived in this country full of hope and who died penniless and alone. But artists leave behind a tangible legacy: their work. Ten De Santis portraits still exist on Columbia's campus. De Santis found most of his customers in the ranks of the chemistry and mining (soon to become engineering) departments. The portraits show distinguished men with luxuriant facial hair, kindly eyes, and the tools of their trade in the frame—test tubes, beakers, and diagrams. Most of the subjects were already dead when painted and De Santis worked from previous portraits or photographs. Former students, alumni, family members, and fellow faculty commissioned or donated them.

I wanted to see what I could in person, and Columbia's Art Properties office obliged. So one cool morning on an early spring day, Lillian Vargas, an administrative assistant in the office, took me on a tour of De Santis's works.

In the university's Miller Seminar Room in Havemeyer Hall, the chemistry building, hangs the portrait of Charles Frederick Chandler, signed by De Santis and dated 1935—the year before the death of the artist. Chandler looks down on the viewer, sporting a bushy walrus mustache and a winged collar, holding a chemistry bottle in his left hand and test tube in his right, as if caught in mid-experiment. Chandler, 1836–1925, was a major figure in modern American chemistry—a former president of New York City's health department who oversaw improvements in protecting the public's welfare. He was a giant on the Columbia faculty, helping establish the School of Mines, serving as dean of the medical and pharmacy schools, and educating generations of chemistry students as a professor.

The portrait, a gift of School of Mines alumni, is apparently a copy by De Santis of a previous one, since Chandler died a good ten years before it was painted. One Columbia curator did not think highly of the copy, writing in 1966 that it was a "considerable error of taste" to hang it instead of the original (no record of that painting was evident), and calling De Santis an "inconsiderable artist." Ouch! The painting underwent other indignities: by the late 1980s, it had suffered punctures and tears resulting from the shooting of paper clips at the surface. In fact, many of the De Santis Columbia paintings endured rough treatment—tears, holes, staining, and the effects of time, like buckling, flaking paint, cracking and deteriorating varnish—mostly the result of normal wear and tear over the decades.

The Art Properties department periodically restored its paintings, including the Chandler, but by early 2017, apart from the two De Santis portraits on display, only three more remained in good condition; the other five were damaged.

Ms. Vargas took me to see the second painting on view. It was a portrait of Thomas Egleston (1832–1900), the founder of the School of Mines. Egleston loomed over the computer and desk in a small administrative office of the Engineering department, the successor to the School of Mines. Egleston, in a crimson academic robe, stares off to the left, seemingly looking out of the window toward Teachers College across 120th Street. The portrait previously had hung over a copying machine in the Egleston Library, where the Chandler painting also lived for a while. The portrait had also made an appearance in the *New York Times* of September 8, 1935. It was used to illustrate a small story announcing the seventy-fifth anniversary celebration of the School of Mines.

Our last stop was Art Properties' storage area, in the basement of Avery. There, Ms. Vargas had set up the other three decently preserved De Santis portraits on easels: the chemistry Professor Thomas Bruce Freas (1868–1928); Henry Drisler, class of 1839 and a professor and dean from 1843 to 1897; and Alexander Holley (1832–1882), a lecturer in the School of Mines who introduced the Bessemer steel process to the United States and wrote frequently for the *New York Times*.

De Santis based the 1934 portrait of Drisler on a photograph. It shows the professor in half-length view, draped in a black satin robe with purple lapel, his florid cheeks fringed by a white mustache-less beard and shaggy sideburns. Two shelves of books rise behind him to his left. Conservators did a good job of fixing some fifteen holes, probably suffered while Drisler hung in Butler Library and also partly the result of paper-clip fire. De Santis presented an early version of the Drisler portrait with a short note to Columbia's president, Nicholas Butler, using quaint and respectful language. "My dear Sir, It would give me great pleasure if you would do me the honor to accept the preliminary painting of your old friend and teacher Dr. H. Drisler, as a token of esteem."

De Santis painted Holley in a gray wool suit, wearing a handlebar mustache, against a pink fabric background. The final portrait on display depicts Professor Freas, holding a slide rule in his right hand and pencil in his left. Paper with a graph drawn on it and a pair of compasses lay on the desk in front of him. Freas looks like Sigmund Freud, with his pointy white beard and round black glasses.

"In its lines and shadings the artist had created the savant," Henry Sherman, a food chemistry professor, told the *Times* in its obituary of De Santis. Faculty opinion, Sherman said, considered the portrait a "remarkably successful job both artistically and as a record of personality." At last report, the portrait had a large hole in the right eye, a puncture on the lower right corner, a tear in the lower left corner, and a slash near the bottom.

Sherman also received the De Santis treatment, portrayed at his desk with a library outside the window near him. So did Eleuterio Felice Foresti (1793–1858), an Italian professor at Columbia who was a revolutionary, jailed by the Austrians for fifteen years before coming to New York; Oliver Wolcott Gibbs (1822–1908), a Columbia grad and chemistry professor at City College and Harvard University; Thomas Henry Harrington (1866–1956); and James Jay (1732–1815), John Jay's brother and a Columbia benefactor. The latter five were the paintings that remained in storage, awaiting some reason, and money, to repair them.

De Santis, the Italian immigrant craftsman, was considered a competent presenter of his august subjects, able to capture an air of wisdom and gravitas but with moments of awkwardness, like imperfectly rendered hands or a head that seemed slightly askew. His handling of fabric also showed skill. For his epoch, he was a contributor to what university administrators considered an important function: preserving the memories of scholarly giants and keeping them in the minds of their intellectual descendants and future generations of students. It is altogether likely that some of his subjects—Chandler and Holley—had Eberhard Faber, the Columbia engineering grad and pencil baron who lived next door to the artist, in their classes. What a lovely example of how the Seven Beauties tied together the lives of people from so many walks of life. How very New York.

As the neighborhood continued to decline, River Mansion changed hands several more times in the 1940s. In 1952, the rooming house was operated by Louise Dickmann, who became something of a heroine to the police. A group of investigators of the State Temporary Rent Commission had been shaking down landlords by taking payoffs in exchange for not reporting violations. Three of the investigators visited Mrs. Dickmann and accused her of overcharging her boarders. They threatened her with fines of more than $10,000. Ah, but for a mere $800, they promised to quash the violations. Mrs. Dickmann marched over to the office of District Attorney Frank S. Hogan, and his investigators set up a sting operation. They prepared a packet of marked bills, and when Ms. Dickmann handed the money over, the three crooked investigators were arrested.

CHAPTER 19.

Farewells

DETECTIVE JOHN OSNATO, THE DOGGED PURSUER of the Rubel gang, retired in June 1944, retreating to a horse farm near Stroudsberg, Pennsylvania, after a life of big investigations and personal tragedies. Along with the death of his first wife in 1916, his son Dudley suffered mental problems and was institutionalized for decades. His son John Jr. was struck by polio as a child. And a third son, Charles, died of appendicitis at age eighteen, three years before Osnato handed in his shield.

Within a year and a half, at the age of fifty-five, the retired lieutenant was dead of a heart ailment. O'Dwyer called him one of his best friends. "He was clever in his work and loyal to his city and friends," he told the *Times*, which ran a eulogistic editorial, suggesting Osnato's death left a final mystery: "What made him what he was?" The answer lay partly in his ability to understand human nature. But other qualities make for great investigators, and the *Times* took the opportunity to muse on what they were: "A taste for danger," or at least the ability to be "sublimely careless of it"; the capacity to think with the deviousness of criminals, speak their language and induce them to talk; and a "faculty for hard, sustained work," both physical and intellectual. Great cops must also have a restless curiosity, a "tenacious mind that can pigeonhole a small, seemingly irrelevant detail for months and even years until it suddenly takes on meaning."

Detective Osnato's funeral mass was held at Our Lady of Angels Roman Catholic Church in Bay Ridge, Brooklyn. More than 200 people attended, including top brass from the police department. He was buried at St. John's Cemetery in Middle Village, Queens.

Fire took an inordinate toll on the property of characters in this tale. It heavily damaged No. 332. A blaze charred much of the Takamines' Japanese décor, and Ahnelt's summer home in New Jersey also went up in flames. Samuel Rubel's mansion in Roslyn, Long Island, suffered the same end in 1946, costing his wife a half-million dollars in jewelry.

Within days of the Rubel verdict, Judge O'Dwyer summoned Burt Turkus, who had represented Stewart Wallace, to his chambers and praised his handling of the Rubel case. "You got everything out of it there was," he said, and then let drop a bombshell: that he planned to run for district attorney. He offered Turkus a staff job if he should be elected. Just a few months later, O'Dwyer won the office, replacing the ineffectual Geoghan, and put Turkus in charge of the homicide division. Working with Osnato, Turkus prosecuted the Murder, Inc., syndicate. O'Dwyer went on to be elected the 100th mayor of New York City in 1945.

For his services, the turncoat Archie Stewart spent fourteen years of his sentence for the Pine Bush robbery stashed away in county jails, to keep him safe from the vengeance of fellow gang members. In 1945, Governor Thomas E. Dewey lopped six years off Stewart's thirty-year sentence as a belated thank-you for his testimony in the Rubel case. But the time spent in the milder county jails proved a mixed blessing. In 1952, the year Stewart was up for parole, the state corrections department asked the New York Attorney General for clarification regarding his status in the penal system. Normally, state prisoners received ten days off of their sentence for good behavior for each month served. But Stewart had spent fourteen years in *county* jails. That raised a question: was Stewart eligible for the time off when his body was in the county lockup while his soul resided in a state prison? The state attorney general said no, a ruling that cost Stewart four years, seven months, one week, and three days of freedom. His bargain with prosecutors did not turn out to be as good a deal as he thought.

In 1942, Dr. Gilbert lost his medical license for failing to report his treatment of McMahon's gunshot wound. Gilbert, who was as outspoken defending himself as trumpeting his treatment of alcoholics, testified in a disciplinary procedure that gang members had threatened to kill him if he went to the police.

The next year, a two-paragraph item in the *Times* reported on the resignation of Bernard Beinstock as an assistant state attorney general. Bienstock, the paper said, had handled a case against Gilbert, who was "indicted for treating wounded members of the Rubel Ice Corporation hold-up gang."

On January 29, the phone rang in the *Times* newsroom. Gilbert was on the line, complaining about that "s" at the end of the word "members." He had treated only one man, he insisted, and he had been told that the man was shot accidentally. True, Gilbert said, he did not report the case, but he thought another doctor had already treated the patient (he made no mention of any threats). In any case, the patient had died before Gilbert could help, he claimed.

Gilbert had other points to make. He said that Francis Madden, the assistant district attorney in the case, obtained the indictment against him but was himself "discredited and disbarred," and that the indictment was eventually tossed out. Gilbert also claimed the Appellate Division allowed him to practice medicine while he fought the criminal charges. A memo to the file on Gilbert in the _Times_'s morgue concludes: "He did not want a correction, but wanted us to go easy on him if his name should come up again and not leave his indictment in the air."

Kress, one of only three people found guilty in the Rubel heist, appealed his conviction. The Appellate Division upheld it by a vote of 3–2, but on the last day of 1940, the New York State Court of Appeals, the higher court, overturned the ruling in a decision that came to be cited for years to come. New York law requires that the state present evidence to corroborate the testimony of an accomplice in a crime. For this reason, something more than Stewart's say-so was needed to prove that Kress took part in the robbery. Barshay introduced two pieces of evidence to fit that bill: the $100 payment passed on from Kress to Stewart, supposedly for the burial of McMahon, and the identification of Kress by Schlayer, the mechanic who said he saw him in the boat during the "test run."

Neither was enough to satisfy the appeals panel.

The law required that the corroborating evidence come from an "independent source of some material fact tending to show that defendant was implicated in the crime." But Kress denied owing Stewart any money. That put the corroborating evidence, that Kress owed money for McMahon's burial, in the mouth of the accomplice, draining it of any independence. The fact of a $100 payment was not enough. "Without establishing the reason for the payment and authority or knowledge and consent of Kress to the payment," it did not count as corroborating, the opinion said.

In the case of Schlayer, nothing showed that he knew about the proposed robbery. He could only state that he saw someone in the boat whom he later identified as Kress, who in turn denied being aboard. "It does not necessarily follow that the presence of Kress in the boat indicated that he took part in the robbery," the court said. "Evil intent cannot be inferred."

Three months later, in March 1941, prosecutors decided not to retry Kress. The indictment was dismissed and Kress was freed.

"My client was discharged," Impellitteri told *The New Yorker* in 1948. "I really thought he was the victim of a frame-up, but what do you think he did? He went out and helped stick up Frank Erickson."

Frank Erickson was a major racetrack bookmaker who had gotten under the skin of Mayor Fiorello LaGuardia. He operated out of a nineteenth-floor suite at the New York Athletic Club, where sums of as much as $100,000 were said to be stored. Around 10:30 a.m. on April 24, 1941, Kress, Stephen Catlin, and Lyman Finnell, an ex-convict who served time in San Quentin and was wanted for parole violations, entered the club, intending to help themselves to Erickson's money. Armed, they carried a leather briefcase filled with black masks, rope, picture wire, handkerchiefs, a roll of cotton, and ammunition as they headed for the elevator to go up to Erickson's suite, 1903-4. But when the elevator door opened on his floor, and the thieves saw Catherine O'Brien, a fifty-two-year-old chambermaid, they decided to improvise. They ordered her to open the suite with her passkey. When she refused, they followed her into a room across the hall, grabbed her, and tried to take hold of the keys. The maid fought back, succumbing only after Kress pistol-whipped her.

In the struggle, the telephone receiver fell off the hook and the switchboard operator heard the fracas. The elevators were halted and a bellboy ran out of the club looking for the police. Two responded: Officer George Schuck, walking his beat at 59th Street and Seventh Avenue, and Officer Charles Kilka, who was writing parking tickets on the block.

Schuck went to call for backup just as the robbers ran down the service stairs. He followed them into the street and ordered them to surrender. They responded with gunfire, and Schuck was wounded. Kress and Catlin headed east on 58th Street, and Finnell west on 59th Street.

A car was waiting at a stoplight, and Finnell jumped in, ordering the driver to hit the gas. Instead, he yanked the keys from the ignition and ran. Finnell went to the car stopped behind, which was driven by a chauffeur with his employer, Mrs. Samuel Solomon of Central Park South, in the back. Finnell slid in next to her and demanded that the chauffeur move—but he too jumped out. Finnell moved into the driver's seat, grabbed the wheel, and began driving. Officer Kilka, his pistol drawn, jumped on the running board. Finnell pointed his gun at his own head and fired, killing himself. The car continued crazily for another fifteen feet, sideswiping two other vehicles and injuring a pedestrian, before coming to a stop, presumably terrifying Mrs. Solomon on the wildest ride of her life.

Meanwhile Catlin disappeared into the coffee shop at the Hotel Maurice, at 145 West 58th Street. Kress was eventually arrested and appeared the next day at a police lineup, a diminished figure in a blue overcoat several sizes too big. During the lineup, he had an exchange with police Captain Fred Zwirz.

After Kress denied involvement, Zwirz said, "You were seen running away from the crime."

"No, I wasn't," Kress answered.

"Were you ever arrested before?" Zwirz asked

"I don't know," said Kress, who had a record of fourteen arrests.

"Would you tell the truth if you knew how?" Zwirz spat out.

Kress replied with a slow shake of his head.

Erickson later gave praise to the chambermaid. "Don't you worry," he said. "I'll take care of her."

Catlin was eventually arrested, tried, and sentenced to life in prison as a repeat offender. Kress pleaded guilty and received a seven-and-a-half- to fifteen-year prison term back at Sing Sing. "I look upon you as one of the finest examples of the fact that crime does not pay," Judge John Mullens said at the sentencing, making a reference to Kress's role as the family black sheep. "You come of a decent family, but you have been 'cutting the corners' of the law for a long time—and getting away with it. I think you are one of the cleverest crooks ever to be arraigned before me, but the law finally caught up with you." He was referring to Kress's long arrest record, including one for the Rubel heist, and limited experience of a prison cell.

Incredibly, after serving his time for trying to rob Erickson and after barely escaping a long prison stretch for the Rubel heist, Kress could not stay out of trouble. He was implicated in the 1955 robbery of a Chase Manhattan Bank branch in Woodside, Queens, that netted $305,000. Even more amazingly, one of his two accomplices was reported to be one Archie Stewart, his old partner in crime and courtroom nemesis. Neither was ever arrested in the robbery. But it is not without some irony that newspaper accounts described the stickup as meticulously planned. It was also called the largest haul of cash from a bank heist in United States history.

As fellow inmates at Alcatraz, John Oley and Percy Geary left behind a voluminous paper trail, probably thanks to Alcatraz's mythic status—inmate records have been carefully kept and are publicly available. Oley stayed at Alcatraz until his transfer to Leavenworth in 1953. He ended up in the penitentiary in Atlanta, from which he was released on parole with incurable cancer on January 5, 1957, having spent nineteen years in federal prison for the kidnapping of Butch O'Connell.

FBI reports obtained under the Freedom of Information Act depict a sad final coda to the life of Oley, the notorious one-time rumrunner, "Legs" Diamond associate, kidnapper, and holdup man.

After his release, Oley returned to his old haunts, living in Ballston Spa, New York, near Albany. He worked for a spell as an instructor for the International Correspondence School. Two years into his newfound freedom, he decided to make a last-ditch effort at generating some income. He called on an old comrade from prison: Eugene Dennis, the general secretary of the Communist Party USA and a well-known figure—he had graced the cover of *Time* magazine in 1949. They were an odd pair, but prison makes for strange connections. Oley was in for kidnapping; Dennis had been sentenced to five years after being convicted under the Alien Registration Act, which proscribed advocating the overthrow of the government.

Dennis was released several years before Oley. But the FBI was still keeping tabs on the Communist official, and Oley made a brief appearance in the surveillance record. On October 9, 1959, shortly before Dennis himself was to receive a diagnosis of lung cancer, Oley showed up at Dennis's office at Communist

Party headquarters at 23 West 26th Street to discuss a possible job at the *Daily Worker*, the Communist Party newspaper. "During this conversation, it was also indicated that Dennis had 'done a lot for John' and his close friends while in prison and that they appreciated it," an FBI report dated January 2, 1959, recounted. (It's not hard to imagine that Dennis provided legal advice, instruction, outside connections, or reading material.) Oley appeared to be deferential, almost sheepish in his request. "He told DENNIS that he realized he should not have come to CP Headquarters as he did not want DENNIS to become involved and promised he would not make a nuisance of himself," another FBI report said.

Dennis could not come through. The *Daily Worker*, already unable to pay existing employees, could not afford to hire him, the party leader said. The FBI agents handling the Dennis surveillance had to make a decision. Should they monitor Oley too? With no job at the party organ, a lack of involvement in Communist politics, and impending mortality, Oley was deemed unworthy of further notice. He died on March 19, 1960, and was buried in St. Mary's Cemetery in Ballston Spa. His widow, Agnes, applied for and received a military headstone, a privilege granted because of Oley's service in the Navy. She chose the cheapest option, a small bronze marker.

Geary's end was even more pathetic. He too served time at the Atlanta penitentiary, having transferred there from Alcatraz in 1955, a fifty-two-year-old convict whose threat to society had run its course. As his release date approached, Geary was apparently overwhelmed by the prospect of surviving on the outside after spending much of his adult life in prison. On July 16, 1959, Percy "Angel Face" Geary, aged fifty-seven, threw himself under the wheels of a prison laundry truck. His chest was crushed. The death certificate listed Josephine Geary as his wife and brewery salesman as his occupation. He was buried in an unmarked grave in Graceland Cemetery in Albany.

Of the rest of the gang, as has been noted, Francis Oley committed suicide, John Hughes disappeared from the face of the earth, and John Manning met his end on an East Harlem Street. As for the first to die, Bernard McMahon? His memory lingered on, but only within his family, and only vaguely. He had no children although two of his siblings did, themselves producing five grand-nieces and grand-nephews. One of the grand-nephews, Tom Worsdale, said the family vaguely knew that Uncle Bernard had somehow gotten mixed up with the Irish mob, leading to his demise. But they never knew the circumstances, and the older generations never discussed Bernard's end. The publication of the hardcover version of this book solved the mystery for them.

And the money that ten men had so carefully planned to steal? As we have seen, Geary and Oley spent much of their shares on lawyers to defend themselves in the kidnapping case. Stewart blew his on the high life. McMahon's was probably passed on to relatives after his death, although Mr. Worsdale said there was never any talk of a sudden influx of wealth. Extortionists apparently relieved Quinn of most of his cut. Where the rest of the cash went, if there was any, is unexplained.

CHAPTER 20.

The Fates of Townhouses: "Life Is Particularly Difficult"

Not twenty years after Nos. 330–337 Riverside Drive were built, the stage was set for their atomization. Landlords took advantage of a change in the housing laws to chop up noble homes into cramped apartments and warren-like rooming houses. The Depression's toll cost people their homes or ruined their ability to pay for large apartments, and many of the townhouses in the area found a market in lodgers sharing bathrooms and kitchens. After World War II, the Upper West Side embarked on an era of decline, and by then the aspirations for Fifth Avenue elegance on Riverside were long gone. Shabbiness and crime marked the following decades. The end of the war also coincided with the close of an era of family ownership of the townhouses on our stretch of Riverside Drive, and also something of a religious conversion. Three of the homes fell out of the hands of clans that had held them for three generations. Two, Nos. 330 and 331, were sold to religious organizations, Buddhist and Catholic.

Yet even as the city's social organization and economy frayed, the Seven Beauties held strong, impassively watching society's changes as they slid into genteel decrepitude. After the unholy destruction of Pennsylvania Station in 1963, the disappearance of old New York seemed ever more possible. Alarmed by the prospect of wiping out old, stately, beloved buildings, in 1965 the city created the Landmarks Preservation Commission, which has the power to protect neighborhoods from the ravages of overdevelopment. Almost immediately, efforts were undertaken to confer landmark status on the seven Riverside Drive buildings as part of a larger protected precinct. The commission established the Riverside-West 105th Street Historic District in 1973, encompassing the Seven Beauties and another twenty-three buildings on 105th Street and one townhouse next door to 337 Riverside Drive.

In the years leading up to landmark status, the Davis-Jephson family played the largest role in keeping the buildings alive. The southern bookend of the row, 330 Riverside Drive, stayed with Lucretia Davis and her husband, George Jephson, until shortly after George died, in 1951. The couple had no children. At his death, Jephson left an estate worth about $5.2 million, including a trust fund for half the amount, which provided income for the rest of Lucretia's life. (Lucretia had her own fortune.) Lucretia outlived her husband by twenty-eight years, dying in Manhattan in 1979 at the age of ninety-three.

Jephson stands out as one of the more decent people to inhabit the Riverside Drive townhouses. He was just the man to spend his life with Lucretia, whose early adulthood was consumed by the bitter separation of her parents. Just one example of his habitual thoughtfulness and courtesy: George wrote a thank-you note to his physical therapist at the New York Athletic Club for his ministrations, assuring him that no offense was ever taken at the man's criticisms and corrections of posture and breathing and that he never caused him any pain. His gestures rose above mere politeness. A bond of affection grew between George and his brother-in-law Harry, Lucretia's beloved sibling. In 1944, when Harry's son Joseph was serving in the Canadian military, Harry became ill and depressed after an unknown illness. George wrote him a letter that is a model of empathy and grace:

"Naturally you think of Joe and the hazards to which he is exposed and you think of a hundred other matters which make the burden hard to bear in addition to the physical discomforts.

"The stress and strain caused by this frightful war has a baneful effect on our minds and nerves and I am no exception. Those who are younger seem to be able to take it in their stride. We who can compare these times with those of former days find it hard to foresee the final outcome and we are therefore greatly depressed when we reflect upon our responsibilities to those we hold dear. We need courage and fortitude and a will to see it through. Brace up Harry. Make up your mind to fight it out and win. Set your mind on getting well and thus co-operate with all those who want you to get well and who are ready to help you in doing it. We will stick it out with you and never let you down."

George went on to write of problems with his business and frustrations and disappointments amid the daily grind. He recalled a story Lucretia told of how Harry would always try to throw a ball over the top of a tall poplar in Montour Falls, the family's home town. "You did it because you were determined to do it. Try to give the same slant on getting well and you will get well." (Harry eventually recovered.)

In 1946, Jephson had established a trust to provide scholarships for college students, and Lucretia Davis, who had never gone to college, left money in her will so that other women would have that opportunity. Donations went to small schools upstate including Keuka College and Cazenovia College, named after the town near Syracuse where Lucretia's father, Robert Davis, the Baking Powder King, built an estate in 1905, the same year he acquired 330 Riverside.

Under Jephson, the Davis concern cemented the ubiquity of its baking powder with lavish advertising. It was selling up to 35 million cans of the stuff by 1934, and more than half of the baking soda sold in the New York area came from Davis. In fact, a federal court said in a trademark case that the name had become almost synonymous with baking powder. Lucretia did not keep the company for long after George's death. Penick & Ford Ltd. bought the business in 1955. Penick itself was gobbled up by R. J. Reynolds in 1965, and the brand was shuttled around corporate America. It most recently belonged to a stable of baking powder brands owned by Clabber Girl of Terre Haute, Indiana—a subsidiary of Hulman & Co.—which also owned, of all things, the Indianapolis Speedway.

Lucretia lived out her final years at the Cazenovia estate in the summer, and in hotels, mainly the Surrey, in New York City in the winter. She frequently bestowed gifts on her friends and relatives—a pendant here, a pocket watch there, cash sums—and set up numerous small trusts for them. A personal thank-you note from President Nixon in 1973 suggests that he too was a recipient of her largesse. An accounting in shaky script of her safe deposit box at an old Chemical Bank branch includes a long list of diamond bracelets, earrings, rings, and brooches, liberally sprinkled with emeralds and sapphires, along with her father's and husband's watches. It is a ledger of opulence. In her final years, Lucretia reworked her will several times to adjust and add various bequests to her circle. At one point, she asked her lawyer how much he would like to inherit. The tactful man demurred, saying it was her decision.

Another attorney, Bob Taisey, who as a young trust and estates lawyer helped handle her legal matters, described Lucretia as a shy, retiring woman, with the naïveté that comes from a long-sheltered life. An opera buff, she had a box at the Metropolitan Opera, occasionally taking lawyers from Taisey's firm to performances after her husband died. Lucretia was not just a patron: she took singing lessons into her eighties.

"The heiress woman I loved and knew as a child was patient and jovial," said Brenda Steffon, her godchild and the daughter of Lucretia's cousin, Joseph Weed. Lucretia had a special affection for Joseph, and paid for his education.

It's hard to know what effect the bitter divorce of her parents had on Lucretia. It was so public, so exhaustively chronicled—a double source of embarrassment for something already so shameful in society. It may have contributed to Lucretia's retreat into a private life.

But three years after her husband's death and well into her sixties, Lucretia made a sudden and unexpected departure from that existence. She married her chauffeur, William Olsen. The marriage shocked and even outraged the circle of family who experienced her benevolence and the friends and lawyers who provided a cocoon of care. Ms. Steffon remembers the phone call at dinner from Lulu telling her parents about the marriage and how stunned they were. "With George gone, she was in a very vulnerable state," Ms. Steffon said. Taisey described Olsen as "self-seeking," and her supporters rallied to try to protect her from what they viewed as a fortune-hunting employee. Lucretia was convinced, and the marriage was quickly annulled. No. 330 may even have been sold to raise money to buy out Olsen.

The Davis name lived on in the courts and the crosshairs of the Internal Revenue Service. In the 1980s, the IRS slapped an $850,000 tax bill on Lucretia's estate, which consisted of stocks and bonds worth about $10 million.

The Jephsons also shaped the fate of the neighboring buildings.

In 1925, George and Lucretia spent $80,000 to buy 331 Riverside Drive, the house next door, where Marion Davies had cavorted with William Randolph Hearst. They repaired the heating system and installed a caretaker to show the place to prospective renters. But because they could not get the rents they wanted, the building remained un-let.

Nine years later, the couple bought 332 Riverside, intending to build an apartment house on the property, which was a possible reason the building was torn down. It is also possible that a fire that seriously damaged the top three floors in 1935 led to the demolition.

At some point, Lucretia also owned 334 Riverside Drive, the site of Bernard McMahon's bloody final moments. In late 1954, she sold Nos. 330 and 331, and the plot at No. 332, to a real estate investor named Fred H. Hill, who opened his firm, the Hansair Realty Corp., in 1948, shortly after being discharged from the army. In 1955, Hill sold 330 Riverside Drive to an arm of the LaSallian Christian Brothers, an international Roman Catholic order focused on education, and No. 331 and the now vacant plot at No. 332 to the American Buddhist Academy. No. 330 later passed from the LaSalle order to another worldwide Catholic organization, Opus Dei, which named it the Riverside Study Center, as a simple plaque next to the door reads.

The center still functions as a Manhattan outpost for Opus Dei, whose members believe that sanctity can be pursued through daily life and work. Opus Dei says it has 90,000 members worldwide and about 3,000 in the United States. Seventy percent live a regular family life and are called supernumeraries. The rest commit themselves to celibacy, and of those there are two categories: numeraries live together in Opus Dei residences, like at No. 330, and associates live separately. Opus Dei, which also has a small body of clergy who adhere to it, was elevated by Pope John Paul II as the Catholic Church's first personal prelature—something like an international diocese—which made it answer directly to the Vatican. With strong influence in the Vatican, a reputation for secrecy, the occasional practice of corporal mortification, and a conservative bent, Opus Dei has become a lightning rod for critics. Its depiction as a nefarious force in Dan Brown's *The Da Vinci Code* popularized suspicions, prompting the order to issue statements pointing out that the book was most definitely a work of fiction.

330 Riverside Drive is home to eight celibate men and three priests, and is a base for organizing activities in the New York City area. Despite the order's international reputation for clandestine influence, which it has worked hard to overcome, a glimpse inside the residence showed a much more mundane—if pious—reality.

On a rainy, foggy Sunday afternoon before a recent Christmas, the residence opened its doors to lay adherents, family, and a few friends for a brief religious ceremony, finger food, and caroling in the large sitting room, once R. B. Davis's library, on the third floor overlooking Riverside Park. The Reverend Malcolm Kennedy, an alarmingly tall and looming priest in a full cassock, played jazz-inflected piano accompaniments to Christmas carols, the titles and page numbers announced by John Coverdale, a tax attorney and a historian of the organization, who is director of the house. Both men live there, along with Brian Finnerty, chief of communications in the United States for Opus Dei; two Opus Dei financial staff members; an administrator and a professor at the Opus Dei–linked business school IESE; a professor at New York University's business school; and a staff member of a non-governmental agency that works with the United Nations. I was there as a visiting journalist.

The afternoon started with a benediction in the exquisitely restored chapel on the second floor, in what used to be the music room, where Lulu probably took her singing lessons and invited musicians gave private recitals. The faithful genuflected in front of the altar, adorned by a cross engraved inside a circle—Opus Dei's symbol of God's presence in the world. About twenty people filled the few rows of pews, bending down on cushioned kneelers; several men who came in later, unable to find spots in the pews, knelt on the bare floor of herring-boned parquet.

After some moments of silent prayer, accompanied by the whispering of a little girl, Father Kennedy and Brian Finnerty swept in. The congregants rose immediately and dropped to their knees. Father Kennedy prayed and delivered a brief homily on the art of rejoicing at Christmas time, tempered with a reminder that penance was also appropriate for the season. The conservative cast of Opus Dei Catholicism was readily apparent in the recitation of Latin prayers and singing of a Latin hymn by Thomas Aquinas, "Adoro te devote." It was a musical moment that would have been pretty anomalous for Jennie and R. B. and Lulu.

Some time later, Finnerty invited me back for a private visit with the architect and architectural historian Seth Joseph

Weine to soak up the spirit of No. 330. Weine summed up the feeling of the carefully restored interior: a Beaux-Arts-ian atmosphere of serenity, conveying "a lion at rest—powerful but not agitated." The dining room has the original heavy furniture, in all its gleaming mahogany—the table, the massive carved buffet, the dining chairs (reupholstered in vinyl, not leather), plus the sylvan murals. It is here the men of Opus Dei take their meals, served by the staff of women. The conservatory still has plants. In the former library, an album of photographs showing the rooms and exterior in the early years of Lucretia and George's marriage sits on a side table.

But the house has a very non-secular feeling of serenity, a quiet but strong contrast with the residence of an industrialist family of a century ago. Statues and paintings of the Virgin Mary dot the rooms. On a hallway wall near the living room, a picture shows John Paul II at the grandiose ceremony in St. Peter's Square declaring Josemaría Escrivá, the organization's founder, a saint. In the former billiard room, a framed verse from the Gospel of John—in Latin—reads: "A new command I give you: Love one another. As I have loved you, so you must love one another. By this everyone will know that you are my disciples, if you love one another." In 2018, Opus Dei undertook extensive renovations of the house, which were continuing into 2019. The tiny fifth-floor rooms were to be enlarged, the service stairs widened, the elevator replaced and private bathrooms installed. But officials promised that the public spaces would remain as they were.

In the lot that once housed No. 332, the New York Buddhist Church built a small structure in 1963 after being forced to leave its home at 171 West 94th Street because of a building development there. A giant bronze statue of Shinran Shonin, the thirteenth-century religious leader who founded the Jodo Shinshu sect of Buddhism, stands on a terrace in front. The statue, which was once situated in a park in Hiroshima and survived the atomic bombing in World War II, was donated by the Japanese businessman Seiichi Hirose, a Jodo Shinshu follower. Shinran gazes benevolently on passersby on Riverside Drive to this day. A dojo operates downstairs. My older son took karate classes there.

The Buddhist Church occupies the second floor in No. 331, using it as a room for receptions and meetings. The minister has an apartment on the fourth floor. The American Buddhist Academy, since renamed the American Buddhist Study Center, operates out of the third floor.

These days, Nos. 333 and 334 are divided into apartments. By 1946, 335 Riverside Drive, the home of the Fabers, was also split up into eight rentals. In 1983, Graciela Chichilnisky, an Argentina-born economist, mathematician, and entrepreneur, bought the building, turning it back into a single-family home, and has bestowed a loving restoration on it over the years.

"I wanted to have a house in New York," Ms. Chichilnisky told me. "I didn't want to have an apartment. It seemed to me that Riverside Drive was the best locale in New York City because it was across the river, and there were no houses in front of it. And there was this beautiful park in front of it. I wanted to have children, and I did, and it was perfect. At the time I didn't realize what I was getting into. You buy a building and say, 'Oh my God, what have I done!'"

In the mid-2000s, Ms. Chichilnisky put No. 335 on the market, at one point listing it for $9.6 million. But she said she changed her mind, finding herself unwilling to part with the house. "Somehow I couldn't come to grips with it," she said. "It was not in the cards." The house where the Fabers lived for so many years had now become part of her bones. "It's who I am. It's part of my life." And so were the ghosts of those who preceded her. Ms. Chichilnisky seemed to share my fascination with forgotten occupants.

"I live with all the people that were there before. They are all there. I don't know how, but they are all there. I have given many parties," she said. But each party felt like "a replay of somebody else's party. This was not my party, this is the continuation of somebody else's."

Next door at No. 336, Mrs. Penfield died at home on September 27, 1944, just as her husband had done twelve years earlier. Her son James Preston Penfield, the last of the family to live there, died on January 26, 1945, at forty-five. Two years later, a granddaughter in Chicago, Margaret Penfield Stockholm, sold the building to the government of Finland to become the residence of the Finnish consul general. Auctioneers had emptied it, putting its array of antiques, reproductions of period furniture, furnishings, and artwork on the block. The contents included oil paintings, bric-a-brac, china, a hundred oriental rugs, and marble statues, all of it in a range of styles—English, French, Georgian, Renaissance, Empire, and Sheraton.

Whether any Finnish consul general ever lived in 336 is unlikely because in 1948 the building passed through several different hands and was eventually broken up into sixteen small apartments. After forty-seven years, the age of 336 Riverside Drive as a single-family mansion was over.

River Mansion, next door, followed a different course. In 1970, after some four decades as a rooming house, the building reverted to a single-family status and became the home of John Mace and his partner Richard Adrian Dorr, a pair of singing teachers who operated the John Mace Music School in the building—even installing a stage on the second floor. In 1978, Edgar Bronfman Jr., the Seagram Co. heir, and his wife Sherry B. Bronfman bought River Mansion with another couple and eventually acquired the whole building. They raised their three children there. Ms. Bronfman, who has since divorced, remains the latest occupant as of this writing.

Ms. Bronfman is friendly with Ms. Chichilnisky and Ms. Bronfman's son works for her. Ms. Bronfman also attended meditation classes at the Buddhist Church. These relationships quickly raised an intriguing question. What connections existed between the previous generations of owners? Did the four long-time families—the Canavans, Penfields, Fabers, and Jephsons, whose residence on the block coincided from the mid-teens to the 1940s—socialize? I can imagine an entire mini-ecosystem of life surrounding the buildings. Maybe the widows Penfield and Canavan formed a friendship and would take regular tea, alternating homes. Perhaps they consulted George Jephson for advice on business matters. Maybe Lothar Faber passed out free pencils to the neighbors, or Jennie Davis worried about the influence of the hot-headed William Canavan on her daughter Lulu before George Jephson came along to provide a respectable match. Marion Davies and her messy establishment may have shocked some of these fine respectable people. Maybe they were all secretly thrilled to have a motion picture star on the block. I can picture Jokichi Takamine rushing over to hold the door for her as she came home with shopping. Some years earlier, Lulu, out for a stroll, may have gazed admiringly on Julia Marlowe when the great actress came bustling home from a long tour, secretly wishing that she could indeed become an actress herself. How did William Randolph Hearst square his newspapers' rabid anti-Japanese campaign with the distinguished Japanese scientist living a few doors away? I'd like to think that one evening, while leaving his love nest, Hearst may have held an umbrella for Takamine as the Japanese gentleman was entering his motorcar in the rain. Perhaps the occupants of these houses returned misdirected mail to each other, or sent servants to borrow sugar, or complained to each other about garbage pickup.

Julia Marlowe's connection to 337 Riverside Drive—later proved, alas, to be erroneous—certainly resonated for the current occupant. Ms. Bronfman, a philanthropist and advocate for arts education and social issues, was an actress herself early in her life. Then Sherri Brewer, she is best known for her role as Marcy, the kidnapped daughter of a crime boss in the blaxploitation movie classic *Shaft*. "Without me Shaft would not have had a job," she said. "I was essential to the plot. He had to find me." Ms. Bronfman also had roles as Ermengarde and Minnie Fay in the all-black cast of *Hello, Dolly!*, starring Pearl Bailey and Cab Calloway, which had a two-year run on Broadway in the 1960s. Ms. Bronfman, who said she was dipping her toe back into the acting world, was moved by the building's sometime association with a great actress of the past. "That meant a lot to me," she said. "I was fascinated by the reality that the woman who owned the house had been an actress and was so successful."

So in the second decade of the twenty-first century on the stretch of Riverside Drive between 105th and 106th streets, here was how things stood. No. 330 belongs to Opus Dei; Nos. 331 and 332 comprise the Buddhist Church. Nos. 333, 334, and 336 are modest apartment buildings. Nos. 335 and 337, River Mansion, have reverted to private ownership. But what about the scene of the Rubel robbery?

A visit one summer day showed that the Rubel Ice Co. building retained its original shape, but with its surface details smoothed out. The six upper windows are no more. They've been bricked up, but ghostly outlines remain. The loading bays are still there, the blue metal rolling doors contrasting with the dark beige stucco wall. The street is quiet. Next to the building are six two-story attached brick houses, on whose stoops witnesses, on that August day in 1934, sat and watched gunmen disguised as peddlers stick weapons in the face of armored guards, round up witnesses, load up bags of cash, and screech away in two cars. The tennis courts are now a parking area for a used car lot. Part of the Rubel property on Cropsey Avenue was also a used car lot.

The building is occupied by the Bruce Supply Co., which makes pipes and sells plumbing products. The main entrance is on the next street over, on the other side of the building, with the address of 8808 18th Avenue. The Rubel robbery was certainly not the last crime associated with the building. A sign attached to the wall near the loading bays offered a $2,000 reward for information leading to the arrest and conviction of the men who robbed the building—in July 2011. Ghostly green photographs, apparently made from night-surveillance cameras, of figures with their shirts pulled over their heads, accompanied the text.

The Bank of Manhattan branch that was the armored car's last port of call, on 86th Street and 20th Avenue, is now a Chase bank, the result of a merger in the 1950s that created Chase Manhattan Bank.

The place near Bay 35th where the getaway boats (one of which was sold at police auction in 1940) might have been moored is no longer accessible, its entrance blocked by a mall. Nearby is the Harbor Motor Inn and a New York Sports Club. A tall aluminum wall blocks the view and access to the water. As for the Ben Machree Boat Club where witnesses saw the Rubel gang make their getaway over the water, an attendant at a fuel oil company nearby said he remembered a boat club being next door years ago. The company may have been on the same site as the fuel oil concern where the witness named Loomis Wolfe in 1934 described one of the getaway boats.

The industrialists who owned the Riverside townhouses are little remembered today, but the products they created or nurtured live on. You can bake with Davis Baking Powder, write with Eberhard Faber pencils, drive on Goodyear tires, brush your teeth with Forhan's Toothpaste, soothe a sour stomach with medicine containing takadiastase, or even watch a Marion Davies movie. As for their homes, the Seven Beauties kept their shapely forms, solid testaments to the real estate cycles of Manhattan, from the hopeful aspirations of the newly rich in a dynamic young economy, to the decline of postwar neighborhoods, to the new prosperity of twenty-first-century gentrification. Going back to their earliest years, not two decades after they were built, the townhouses already reflected the character that could always be found in Manhattan's Upper West Side: The respectable and upright mixed with the seamy and sordid, bridged somehow by the bohemian and artistic. That really has always been the promise of New York City, an egalitarian stew.

Why did I pick these buildings in which to take up mental residence for so long? On the surface, it was pretty convenient. I was lucky enough to live around the corner from the oldest remaining freestanding row of townhouses on Riverside Drive, in a district that had been declared a landmark. I had also spent my childhood in close proximity. They were part of my inner landscape, and their European elegance and charm, their sense of the past, somehow touched in me a longing for another world, or a world gone by. The writer Dawn Powell expressed a similar feeling in a journal entry of 1962: "Riverside Drive lovely and pink and melancholy as Youth for it represents my youth."

On another level, the research into their histories came from a deep love of New York City—not just the life here but my life here and the visual backdrop all around it. It was refreshing to stay close to home, mentally, after part of a journalism career focused on the world. Traveling to the past, which existed in a very manifest way in the form of brick and stone, provided respite from the onrush of the digital future that has flooded our daily life. Maybe memorializing past lives helped soothe some creeping midlife anxiety about rounding Dante's curve into middle age and that thing that comes after it. I hope I have reclaimed some of the lives of those who passed through the rooms of one row of seven townhouses on the edge of America, shades flitting by like falling blossoms and blowing leaves.

Chronology

1890 —William Ahnelt arrives in the United States
1900 —Jokichi Takamine isolates adrenaline
1901 —Gangsters John Oley and Percy Geary are born
     —Julia Marlowe has her first big hit on Broadway,
     When Knighthood Was in Flower
1902 —330–337 Riverside Drive are completed
1903 —Samuel Rubel immigrates to the United States
     —Julia Marlowe buys 335 Riverside Drive
     —Mary Donnell buys 333 Riverside Drive
1904 —Northward extension of the IRT subway opens
1905 —Robert B. Davis buys 330 Riverside Drive
1906 —Julia Marlowe sells 335 Riverside Drive
1907 —Mary Donnell dies
1909 —Jokichi Takamine buys 334 Riverside Drive
1910 —Riverside Park completed.
     —R. B. Davis sues Jennie Davis for divorce
     —Canavan family buys 333 Riverside Drive
1913 —Rubel Coal and Ice Company by now founded
1914 —David Canavan, owner of 333 Riverside, dies at
     forty-seven
1915 —Jennie Weed Davis dies in Santa Monica,
     California

—Lucretia Davis and George Jephson marry

—Marion Davies and William Randolph Hearst meet

1916 —Julia Marlowe retires from the stage

—David Canavan, owner of No. 333, dies

1917 —Marion Davies's first film, *Runaway Romany*, is released

1918 —William Ahnelt sells 331 Riverside Drive; Marion Davies moves in

1920 —Prohibition, the racketeer's jobs program, begins

1921 —Jokichi Takamine sells 334 Riverside Drive to Richard Forhan; Takamine dies the next year

1922 —Filmed version of *When Knighthood Was in Flower* makes Marion Davies a star

1925 —Davies moves out of 331 Riverside Drive

1931 —Jack "Legs" Diamond killed in an Albany rooming house

1932 —Raymond Penfield dies

1933 —21st Amendment ratified, ending Prohibition

—John "Butch" O'Connell kidnapped in Albany

—Richard Forhan sells 334 Riverside Drive to a realty company

1934 —Rubel armored car heist takes place in Bath Beach, Brooklyn

1936 —John Manning is murdered

—Artist Michael De Santis dies

1937 —Geary and Oley convicted of O'Connell kidnapping

1938 —Rubel indictment handed up

1939 —Rubel trial takes place

1941 —Jack Alexander, the Rubel heist's chronicler, writes the article that introduces Alcoholics Anonymous

1945 —James Preston Penfield, last of the family at 336 Riverside Drive, dies

1955 —Saul Bellow writes his novel *Seize the Day* at 333 Riverside Drive

1957 —John Oley released from prison

1960 —John Oley dies at fifty-nine

1963 —New York Buddhist Church builds small structure on site of 332 Riverside Drive

1968 —Columbia University student Pauline Sargent, of 334 Riverside Drive, becomes first person jailed in campus protest there

1977 —Daniel O'Connell, the Albany political boss, dies at ninety-one

1979 —Lucretia Davis, the owner of 330 Riverside Drive, dies at ninety-three

Acknowledgments

THIS BOOK WOULD NOT HAVE COME about without Constance Rosenblum. Doubly so. As editor of the City Weekly section at the *New York Times*, Connie published the story that served as its kernel. Then, years later, she read a rudimentary manuscript and was unflinching in her encouragement that it could be a book. She should know—she's written a few volumes about New York City herself, and has moved on to a second career as a book doctor. The other major source of encouragement was my agent and fellow Dutchman Andrew Blauner, who stayed the course on a twisty route through the publishing world. And special thanks to Lilly Golden, my editor at Skyhorse, who from the start was a calm presence and expert guide through the byways of book publishing.

In the researching of the book, I owe a debt of gratitude to Brenda Steffon, the granddaughter of Harry Weed (Jennie Davis's brother), who was extraordinarily generous in opening up her family's archives, giving me access to letters, legal documents, and appraisals—and entrusting those materials to me. Her friend, photographer Julia Kracke, was also helpful in making copies of Davis/Weed family photographs. Current owners and occupants lent me their time and memories: Graciela Chichilnisky at No. 335, Sherry Bronfman at No. 337, and Brian Finnerty at No. 330. I extend thanks to Ben

Gocker at the Brooklyn Public Library's Brooklyn Collection and Ellen Belcher at Special Collections of the Lloyd Sealy Library of John Jay College of Criminal Justice, who were helpful in directing me to information about the Rubel heist and related matters. At Columbia, thanks also to Jocelyn K. Wilk, archivist at the Columbia University Rare Book & Manuscript Library, and Roberto C. Ferrari, the curator of Art Properties. Sean Malone pointed out invaluable sources for life among the Fabers at 335 Riverside.

Warm thanks also to my neighbors and neighborhood history lovers, Nancy Macagno, Al Berr, Jim Mackin, Gil Tauber, and Gary Dennis.

There is a common saying that every journalist has a book inside and that's where it should stay. My friends at the *Times*, especially my lunchtime gang at the big round cafeteria table known as "The Table," ignore this with great gusto, and have served as book-writing inspiration, journalistic role models, and great company over the years. One of them, Jeff Roth, the maestro of the morgue, was incredibly helpful in securing archival photographs. Special thanks also to my editors over the years at the *Times*, especially Jonathan Landman and Jim Oestreich. And I extend my appreciation to Arthur O. Sulzberger, Jr., and the Sulzberger family for keeping the *Times* enterprise alive and healthy.

Justin Davidson, who knows and writes about New York as well as anyone alive, also deserves my gratitude for his brains and friendship, and for immeasurably improving the manuscript—in its prose and organization. He aided in drawing connections I didn't know were there. My colleague Michael Kimmelman helped shape my conception of cities and the City. Laurence Beckhardt, a best friend with whom I have been exploring this city since high school, came with me to the scene of the Rubel crime. My cousin Eric Wakin, a historian and archivist, was a clear-eyed sounding board. My son Thomas Wakin was an early reader of the manuscript, offering sharp-eyed and unbiased suggestions. In a funny sort of way, he and his brother Michael were inspirations for a book that in the end was about the passage of time and what we leave behind. My deepest debt of all, as a writer and as a person, goes to my wife and close reader, Vera Haller.

A Note on Sources

THE MORE THE JOURNALIST'S WORLD BECOMES a digital marketplace—where a reporter's life is increasingly lived on Twitter and Facebook, where stories exist as URLs, and where we seek audience through multimedia and audiovisual pieces—the more acute grow the pangs of nostalgia for any lover of that artifact known as a printed newspaper. Don't get the wrong idea. While I still regularly peruse printed papers, I have moved on. My journalistic existence, like that of most people in the field, is largely online now.

But oh, those clips! They are actual things (even if read in digital form) beamed to us from another age: the crammed-together stories, crowded headlines, ghostly photographs of men with slicked hair and coiffed women with pearls. And they include so much detail, including street addresses for people in the news. Without that, my task in chronicling the lives of the people in our townhouses on Riverside Drive would have been much more difficult. The papers—the *New York Times, Brooklyn Eagle*, the *New York Tribune* and the *New York Herald-Tribune, Evening World, New York Sun, New York Post, New York Daily News*—served as the backbone for much of my research into the townhouses and especially the story of the Rubel heist, with a supporting account from the decision by New York State's Appellate Division upholding the Kress conviction.

Also invaluable for the Rubel heist was the two-part _New Yorker_ series by Jack Alexander and two co-writers, Carroll Moore on the first article and Charles Bender on the second, published a month before the trial. I drew heavily on it for the story up until then. The newspapers also chronicled the ups and downs of Samuel Rubel and his ice and coal business.

Information about the backgrounds of Percy Geary and John Oley also came from their FBI files, obtained via a Freedom of Information Act request, and their Alcatraz prison files. William Kennedy's _O Albany!_ helped with their early criminal careers, as did Frank S. Robinson's _Machine Politics_. The original trial record of the O'Connell kidnapping case, courtesy of the National Archives, provided details and the opportunity to actually hold the ransom notes in my hand.

The architect and historian Seth Joseph Weine provided me with a crash course in Beaux-Arts building design and helped inform my descriptions of the townhouses.

Census records helped establish who lived where and with whom. _The Real Estate Record and Builder's Guide_ is an invaluable treasure trove for anyone writing about New York City buildings. Russell Shorto's book about the Dutch days of New York, _The Island at the Center of the World_, and the New York City Landmarks and Preservation Commission designation of the block as a landmark district provided historical context for our Seven Beauties. The same can be said for Burrough and Wallace's _Gotham_.

Benardo and Weiss's _Brooklyn By Name_ helped with the story of Bath Beach; Gado's _Death Row Women_ gave me the Scarnici quote about doublecrossing; the Nasaw and Guiles books served me well for the story of No. 331 and its connection to Marion Davies, William Randolph Hearst's mistress. For the early years of No. 334, the Takamines' residency there, and the corporate history of his successor company, the website enzyme-facts.com was helpful. The Soyinfo Center's William Shurtleff and Akiko Aoyagi produced an incredible trove of information on the Japanese scientist with their online publication that contains a summary of just about every published work, document and record related to him. Takamine is a fascinating, if forgotten, figure who deserves more attention.

Members of the Ellington family—Stephen and Michael James and Mercedes Ellington—were very helpful and generous with their time in reconstructing the Duke's history at the townhouses. I also drew upon interviews in the Duke Ellington Oral History project at Yale University.

For No. 333, Mark Geiger's work in his dissertation at the University of Missouri-Columbia uncovered fascinating details about the life of the Donnells. The Faber corporate website helped trace back numerous generations of Fabers, with the devilishly repetitive first names of Lothar and Eberhard.

Another historical figure in the Takamine category of worthy-of-resurrection is Julia Marlowe, who ruled the stage and newspaper columns in her day but receives little recognition in our time. Her story was constructed from the several books cited in the bibliography.

Bibliography

Benardo, Leonard, and Jennifer Weiss. *Brooklyn By Name: How the Neighborhoods, Streets, Parks, Bridges, and More Got Their Names.* New York: New York University Press, 1999.

Bennett, Joan. "Adrenalin and Cherry Trees." *Modern Drug Discovery,* December 2001.

Blumenthal, Ralph. *Miracle at Sing Sing: How One Man Transformed the Lives of America's Most Dangerous Prisoners.* New York: St. Martin's Press, 2004.

Burrows, Edwin G., and Mike Wallace. *Gotham: A History of New York City to 1898.* New York: Oxford UP, 2000.

Clark, James Gregory. *History of William Jewell College, Liberty, Clay County, Missouri.* St. Louis: Central Baptist Print, 1893.

Clark, Neil G. *Dock Boss: Eddie McGrath and the West Side Waterfront.* Fort Lee, N.J.: Barricade Books, Inc., 2017

Davies, Marion, edited by Pamela Pfau and Kenneth S. Marx. *The Times We Had: Life with William Randolph Hearst.* New York: Ballantine, 1975.

de Mille, Agnes. *Where the Wings Grow.* Garden City, NY: Doubleday, 1978.

Dolkart, Andrew S. *Morningside Heights: A History of Its Architecture and Development.* New York: Columbia UP, 1998.

English, T. J. *Paddy Whacked: The Untold Story of the Irish-American Gangster.* New York: Regan, 2005.

Fuenfhausen, Gary G. *A Guide to Historic Clay County, Missouri: Architectural Resources and Other Historic Sites of the Civil War.* Kansas City, MO: Little Dixie Publications, 1999.

Gado, Mark. *Death Row Women: Murder, Justice, and the New York Press.* Westport, CT: Praeger, 2008.

Geiger, Mark W. "Missouri's Civil War: Financial Conspiracy and the Decline of the Planter Elite, 1861–1865." Diss. 2006.

Guiles, Fred Lawrence. *Marion Davies: A Biography.* New York: McGraw-Hill, 1972.

Irving, Washington. *A History of New York by Diedrich Knickerbocker.* New York: G. P. Putnam's Son, 1902.

Kennedy, William. *Billy Phelan's Greatest Game.* New York, NY: Penguin, 1983.

Kennedy, William. *O Albany!: Improbable City of Political Wizards, Fearless Ethnics, Spectacular Aristocrats, Splendid Nobodies, and Underrated Scoundrels.* New York: Viking, 1983.

Kisseloff, Jeff. *You Must Remember This: An Oral History of Manhattan from the 1890s to World War II.* Baltimore, MD: Johns Hopkins UP, 1999.

Marlowe, Julia, and E. H. Sothern. *Julia Marlowe's Story.* New York: Rinehart, 1954.

Nasaw, David. *The Chief: The Life of William Randolph Hearst.* Boston: Houghton Mifflin, 2001.

Okrent, Daniel. *Last Call: The Rise and Fall of Prohibition.* New York: Scribner, 2010.

Osnato, John. *Lawyer in the House.* New York: Vantage, 1994.

Petroski, Henry. *The Pencil: A History of Design and Circumstance.* New York: Knopf, 1990.

Putnam, Peter. Cast Off the Darkness. New York: Harcourt, Brace and Company, 1957.

Reynolds, Quentin. Headquarters. New York: Harper & Brothers, 1955.

Riverside-West 105th Street Historic District Designation Report. New York City Landmarks Preservation Commission, 1973.

Robinson, Frank S. Machine Politics: A Study of Albany's O'Connells. New Brunswick, NJ: Transaction, 1977.

Russell, Charles Edward. Julia Marlowe, Her Life and Art. New York: D. Appleton, 1926.

Salwen, Peter. Upper West Side Story: A History and Guide. New York: Abbeville, 1989.

Salter, James. Burning the Days: Recollection. New York: Random House, 1997.

Shattuck, Charles Harlen. Shakespeare on the American Stage. Washington: Folger Shakespeare Library, 1976.

Shurtleff, William and Aoyogi, Akiko. Jokichi Takamine (1854–1922) and Caroline Hitch Takamine (1866–1954): Biography and Bibliography. Soyinfo Center, 2012.

Shorto, Russell. The Island at the Center of the World: The Epic Story of Dutch Manhattan and the Forgotten Colony That Shaped America. New York: Doubleday, 2004.

Stratemann, Klaus. Duke Ellington Day by Day and Film by Film. Copenhagen: JazzMedia, 1992.

True, Clarence, compiler. Riverside Drive. New York: Press of Unz & Co., 1899.

Turkus, Burton B., and Feder, Sid. Murder, Inc.; The Story of the Syndicate. New York: Da Capo Press, 1992.

Waller-Zuckerman, Mary Ellen. "'Old Homes, in a City of Perpetual Change': Women's Magazines, 1890–1916." The Business History Review, vol. 63, no. 4, 1989, pp. 715–756, www.jstor.org/stable/3115961.

Ward, Nathan. *Dark Harbor: The War for the New York Waterfront.*
New York: Farrar, Straus and Giroux, 2010.

White, Norval, and Elliot Willensky. *AIA Guide to New York City.*
New York: Crown, 2000.

*The WPA Guide to New York City: The Federal Writers' Project Guide
to 1930s New York.* New York: Pantheon, 1982.